Literature, Medicine, Health

VOLUME 19 NUMBER 2 2019

Moving Worlds is a biannual international magazine. It publishes creative, critical, literary, and visual texts. Contributions of unpublished material are invited. Books for notice are welcome. Manuscripts should be double-spaced with footnotes gathered at the end, and should conform to the MHRA (Modern Humanities Research Association) Style Sheet. Wherever possible the submission should be in Word for Windows, sent as an attachment. Please include a short biography, address, and email contact.

Moving Worlds is an internationally refereed journal based at the University of Leeds and Nanyang Technological University.

The editors do not necessarily endorse the views expressed by its contributors.

Moving Worlds is a Green Open Access journal.

All correspondence – manuscripts, books for review, enquiries – should be sent to: The Editor, *Moving Worlds*, School of English, University of Leeds, Leeds LS2 9JT, UK

email: mworlds@leeds.ac.uk
http://www.movingworlds.net
https://www.facebook.com/pages/Moving-Worlds/146855128711860?fref=ts

SUBSCRIPTION RATES FOR 2019
Individuals: 1 year £32.00 includes postage
Institutions: 1 year £62.00 includes postage
Students: 1 year £14.00 includes postage
Cheques should be made payable to: University of Leeds (Moving Worlds)
Payment is accepted by Visa or Mastercard, please contact Moving Worlds for details

Published by *Moving Worlds*
at School of English
University of Leeds
Leeds UK
LS2 9JT

with Division of English
Nanyang Technological University
Singapore 637332

ISBN 978-0-9935316-7-5   ISSN 1474-4600

Printed in the UK by Imprint Digital, Exeter

Contents

Acknowledgements

Moving Worlds is published with funding assistance from the School of English, University of Leeds. UK, and School of Humanities, NTU, Singapore.

UNIVERSITY OF LEEDS

We would like to thank all the contributors to this journal.

The symbolic image of braces that are placed on the teeth for correction © istock / dimapf, p. 55.

Cover picture: Solomon Enos, 'Forest Encryptor', from the work *From Stars to Stars: An Indigenous Perspective on Human Evolution* (2012) acrylic, enamel, china markers on asphalt saturated felt, 36" (w) x 108" (t) Photo credit: Shuzo Uemoto

All further picture credits are included in the texts

Moving Worlds
Forthcoming issues include:

Translations
Postcolonial Futures

All titles subject to confirmation

Editorial

CLARE BARKER

The image on the cover of this issue of *Moving Worlds* is part of *Polyfantastica*, a vast series of works of Pacific science fiction and fantasy by the gifted Native Hawaiian artist, Solomon Enos. Set in a parallel universe whose narrative timelines reach 40,000 years into the future, and realized in a range of media from sculpture to the graphic novel, *Polyfantastica* charts the physical and cultural evolution of indigenous Pacific civilizations that, in this paraverse, have never been colonized and whose science and technology eventually enable space travel and the development of collective human consciousness. A futuristic human figure – although not necessarily recognizably so – our cover image provocatively suggests states of embodied, cognitive, and emotional difference. It speaks to the human body's capacity for adaptation and evolution; its power, fragility, and often strangeness; and the sense of hope and futurity that is always implicated in developments in medicine and biotechnology. It is with such a spirit of imagination and curiosity regarding human embodiment and health that this issue of *Moving Worlds* on 'Literature, Medicine, Health' is conceived.

The articles gathered together in this issue reflect the diversity and strength of research currently being undertaken in the medical or health humanities. The field of medical humanities has recently undergone a critical turn, its concerns expanding from its predominantly Anglo-American knowledge base and its concentration on the 'primal scene' of encounter between physician and patient – a scene focused on communications and miscommunications between individual actors – to a new sense of urgency regarding the importance of registering health and medicine's investment, and 'entanglement', in many other spheres of experience and critique.[1] Critical explorations of health and medicine across cultures and in relation to race, class, gender, disability and economics are not the least of these concerns.

Several of the articles in this issue began life in a series of panels on global and postcolonial approaches to health at the second congress of the UK's Northern Network for Medical Humanities Research, held in Leeds in September 2018. Joined by our colleagues from Nanyang Technological University, Singapore, the resulting issue offers rich insights into health concerns and medical treatment across cultures. Medicine and health are necessarily transcultural formations, particularly in developing nations, given the ways that global health governance (such as World Health Organization initiatives and health-focused Sustainable Development Goals) intersects with national health services and local policies and initiatives. Collectively, the articles in 'Literature, Medicine, Health' explore literary texts that take us to Singapore, Aotearoa New Zealand, the Marshall Islands, Zimbabwe, the United States, Rwanda, the rainforests of the Amazon, and Ghana. They confront us with, among many other concerns, the health implications of postcolonial politics; the entanglement of medicine with the processes and infrastructure of globalization; and the connections between environment, ecology, and health in a climate-changing world.

Katherine Hindley's article takes us back to a founding figure in Western medicine, Hippocrates, to show how literary texts can trouble the boundaries between faith and science, miracle and medicinal cure. Such concerns are echoed in several contributions focused on the contemporary period, in which tensions surface between 'Western' allopathic medicine, global health systems, and other traditions of medicinal knowledge and treatment. Amy Rushton explores the gap between Western psychiatric models and culturally located manifestations of distress in Tsitsi Dangarembga's long-awaited recent novel, *This Mournable Body*, the final instalment in the acclaimed *Nervous Conditions* trilogy. Veronica Barnsley analyses tensions between neoliberal global health policies and traditional midwifery practices in *The Housemaid* by Ghanaian novelist, Amma Darko. Emily Timms's article on *Chappy* by Māori author, Patricia Grace, engages with indigenous perspectives on ageing in order to critique 'successful ageing' strategies within international health policy. Clare Barker discusses the exploitation of indigenous traditional ecological knowledge (TEK) by pharmaceutical corporations in contemporary 'biopiracy' narratives. The powerful poem, 'Monster', by Marshallese poet and climate activist, Kathy Jetñil-Kijiner, weaves together statistics on birth defects caused by nuclear testing in the Pacific with the narrative of a demonic female figure, Mejenkwaad, from Marshallese legend, and Michelle Keown's analysis of Jetñil-Kijiner's work considers ways in which creative reinterpretations can bring critical perspectives on Pacific nuclear histories to new audiences.

The contributions to this issue span genres in creative and fascinating ways. Madeleine Lee's sequence of witty bite-sized poems about teeth bring to attention the everyday experiences of living with our vulnerable, unpredictable, often imperfect bodies, and their impact on our sense of self and personhood. Avaes Mohammad's short fiction, 'Four Steps to

Immunity', reveals the impact on families of caring duties when relatives often have conflicting physical and emotional needs. Not surprisingly, given the centrality of pathographies to critical work in medical humanities, several articles focus on life writing. Graham Matthews' article explores the culturally specific nuances of breast cancer memoirs in multicultural, multilingual Singapore, including the appeal of alternative therapies. Michelle Chiang analyses the life writing of people with terminal diagnoses and argues that early conversations about our end of life preferences can be beneficial for all of us. Frances Hemsley's article focuses on the testimonial memoir of an NGO manager dealing with outbreaks of epidemic illness in the wake of the Rwandan genocide, and explores the complex layers of ethnic, political, and moral meaning attached to diseased bodies in this context.

This issue begins with Simon Armitage's 'Finishing It', a poem inscribed like a charm on a chemotherapy pill, a 'sugared pill / of a poem' that 'speaks ill / of illness itself'. Literature, these short lines suggest, can denounce the injustices and indignities of disease, can express the hopes and fears encapsulated in new biotechnologies, can celebrate the miraculous curative powers of medicine, can itself have healing properties. From Virginia Woolf's meditations on the 'daily drama of the body', and the 'undiscovered countries' of the soul that illness discloses to Susan Sontag, literature has always had the power to illuminate the mental, embodied, and spiritual aspects of health and illness and interrogate the complexity of concerns that illness brings.[2] It is also able to expose the power relations built into medical care, the inequalities at work in healthcare services, and the infrastructural issues that dictate priorities in medical research. In its creative and critical writings, 'Literature, Medicine, Health' embraces these multiple valences of health and medicine, collectively helping to imagine more equitable health futures and to map patterns of exploitation and care across the moving worlds we inhabit.

NOTE

1. Anne Whitehead and Angela Woods, 'Introduction', in *The Edinburgh Companion to the Critical Medical Humanities*, eds, Anne Whitehead and Angela Woods (Edinburgh: Edinburgh UP, 2016), pp. 1-31 (p. 2).
2. Virginia Woolf, 'On Being Ill', *The New Criterion*, January 1926, 32-45, pp. 32, 33. Susan Sontag, *Illness as Metaphor and AIDS and Its Metaphors* (London: Penguin, 1991).

SIMON ARMITAGE

Finishing It

I can't configure
a tablet
chiselled by God's finger

or forge
a scrawled prescription,
but here's an inscription, formed

on the small white dot
of its own
full stop,

the sugared pill
of a poem, one sentence
that speaks ill

of illness itself, bullet
with cancer's name
carved brazenly on it.

Commissioned by the Institute of Cancer Research in recognition of on-going progress
in drug-based cancer treatment.

Speaking to *The Guardian* on his poem engraved on the chemotherapy pill, an emblem of the new drugs to treat the disease which the Institute of Cancer Research hopes to develop, Simon Armitage notes that 'Science and poetry are closer associates than many people assume ... [a]nd like science, poetry is a "what if" activity, imagining outcomes and possibilities based on creative thinking.

'I liked the sense that poem and pill might collaborate to produce both a medical and emotional cure, and that something so minimalist could aim to bring down something so enormous and destructive.'

The Guardian, Interview, 14 August 2019,

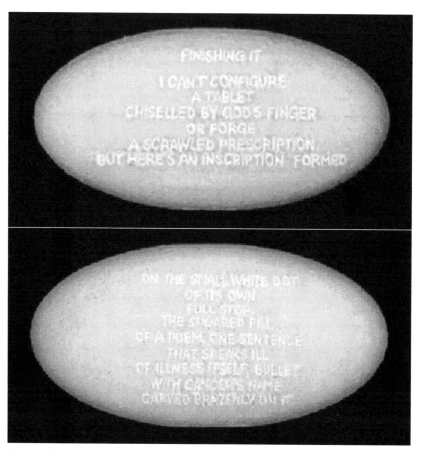

Engraved into a standard sized pill by micro-artist Graham Short. Photograph credit John Angerson.

Cancer Narratives in Singapore: Uncertainty and Risk in the Medical Encounter

GRAHAM MATTHEWS

Introduction

The word 'pathography' first appeared in 1848 when it referred to an account or description of a disease written by a physician observing a patient (OED s.v. *pathography*). By the late-twentieth century, however, the term was increasingly used to allude to the expanding genre of personal narratives of illness and dying authored by doctors, patients, caregivers and novelists. Autobiographies and biographies that describe illness highlight the myths and metaphors that inform the ways health and sickness are perceived. They offer insight into what it is like to live with a critical or chronic illness, and express the ambiguities and uncertainties of the patients' conditions in ways that extend beyond biological and scientific perspectives.

Scholars in the medical humanities have adopted a variety of critical approaches to illness narratives. Anne Hunsaker Hawkins views pathographies as 'illustrative of cultural myths, attitudes, and assumptions about various aspects of the illness experience' while Lisa Diedrich locates their importance in their ability to describe 'both particular, individual experiences of illness, as well as the ways that illnesses, such as tuberculosis, AIDS, and breast cancer, become cultural and political events'.[1] Arthur Frank identifies distinct archetypes including the restitution narrative, chaos narrative, and quest narrative, while Arthur Kleinman and Howard Brody strive to restore the patient's voice to the medical encounter.[2] Stella Bolaki widens the analysis of illness narratives to include photography, film, performance, and theatre, and numerous commentators have devoted critical attention to the history of the genre and the ways in which illness narratives present illness as immutably bound to issues of race, gender, class, and sexuality.[3] To date, however, there has been limited critical engagement with illness narratives in Singapore and Southeast Asia.

Health, sickness, and conceptions of care, suffering, and risk signify in very different ways within different cultures and societies. The meaning of sickness is further influenced by diverse religious, linguistic, philosophical, and literary traditions. Consequently, it is important to uncover existing stories of sickness and to foster fresh engagements with various local and regional conceptions of medicine and healing. In this article, I provide an overview of the development of pathographies in multilingual, multicultural Singapore with a specific focus on the sub-genre of cancer narratives.

As with many critical illnesses, a cancer diagnosis is not only a traumatic event that disrupts the equilibrium of the body but causes a significant shift in socio-cultural identity: 'it is precisely the change in the average everydayness of their lives wrought by illness or injury that matters most to patients'.[4] As Frank states,

> critical illness leaves no aspect of life untouched ...Your relationships, your work, your sense of who you are and who you might become, your sense of what life is and ought not to be – these all change, and the change is terrifying.[5]

In the face of the body's dysfunction, and the cold, detached perspective of the biomedical model, which reduces the individual to the level of an object, medical humanities scholars are prompted to emphasize the phenomenological experience of sickness. They explore the ways in which patients turn to narrative to restructure their sense of self in ways that facts and statistics cannot. In this article, I draw on a range of texts to identify tendencies in the cultural construction of cancer in Singapore. Individual texts are not evaluated on their literary merits but read for the insights they offer into the experience of critical illness in Singapore. Although it is possible to read an account as biased, misleading, or ideological, it nevertheless tells the truth of an individual's personal experience; in this respect, illness narratives deliver an emotional truth rather than simply a factual one.

Illness narratives in Singapore

Since 1990, Singaporeans have published more than a hundred pathographies which, spanning novels, short stories, memoirs and poetry, are dedicated to conditions such as cancer, diabetes, HIV/AIDS. In addition, more than twenty Singaporean plays foreground health and sickness including Haresh Sharma's *Off-Centre* (1993), Paddy Chew's *Completely With/Out Character* (1999), and Stella Kon's *The Bridge* (1992). There was a dramatic increase in the number of pathographies describing mental health conditions, such as depression, autism, bipolar disorder, dementia and schizophrenia, published in the wake of the National Mental Health Blueprint initiative (2007-2012) by the Institute of Mental

Health (IMH). Although the majority of these stories were written by Chinese Singaporeans, authorship since 2010 has become more diverse with testimony from Malay, Indian, and Eurasian ethnic groups. The space for such testimony has become more extensive with charities and clinics, such as Club Heal and Parkway Cancer Centre, publishing pathographies, and further testimonials are available on the Singapore Cancer Society website. In its turn, the book series, *Shattered We Heal* (2014-2015), gives voice to persons with mental health problems, and seeks to offer assistance to community integration efforts as well as eradicate stigma. Narratives about the experience of living with HIV/AIDS are to be found in the novels *Peculiar Chris* (1992) by Johann Lee, *Different Strokes* (1993) by David Leo, and the collection, *I Will Survive* (2013), dedicated to expressing the diversity of gender and sexuality in Singapore.

Local Singaporean pathographies must be situated in relation to broader global trends. As part of such a project, which set out to create a resource to assist scholars to develop more granular studies of this complex and evolving genre, a team of research assistants at Nanyang Technological University helped to compose a comprehensive taxonomy of Singaporean illness narratives. Ongoing analysis of these narratives highlights (i) the subjective experience of health and sickness, including the social realm of plans abandoned and abilities impaired; (ii) the myths and metaphors attached to various health issues; (iii) the ways in which the daily life of a caregiver challenges their ideals, stretches emotional limits, and heightens interdependency; (iv) the ways in which scientific medicine and alternative medicines are perceived by patients and their families. The act of telling stories of sickness helps raise awareness of the social, psychological, and familial impact of illness and serves to restore the voice of the patient which is often lost amid biomedicine's singular focus on the body and disease. Pathographies are typically organized in terms of disease categories and the most common in Singapore is the cancer narrative. This article draws on the findings of the Singapore Illness Narratives project to examine cancer narratives that engage with the cultural constructions of health and sickness in Singapore. These texts shed light on a range of issues such as doctor–patient relations, the impersonality of biomedicine, the appeal and the dangers of alternative therapies, and the impact of a cancer diagnosis on the family, employment, and faith.

In *Reconstructing Illness* Hawkins provides a taxonomy of 156 American cancer narratives for the period 1973-1998. Out of these, fifteen include direct reference to God and the Christian faith. By contrast, all seventeen Singaporean English-language cancer narratives invoke religious faith in varying degrees and some of the stories double as conversion narratives as the patient turns to God for solace in the face of overwhelming fear and uncertainty. These narratives are known as testimonials: 'public professions of faith that are meant to bear witness to the truth and strengthen other believers by relating an experience of spiritual trial or conversion'.[6] Voices from the Muslim, Buddhist, Taoist, and Hindi religious communities are currently absent. To date, cancer narratives in English are mostly written by Chinese-Singaporeans. Further exploration may uncover stories written in other languages but the current survey suggests that there is a need to promote the writing of fictional and non-fictional illness narratives from under-represented groups.

Singaporean cancer narratives tend to be uncritical of biomedicine yet the uncertainty of prognosis and treatment lead some to seek alternative health practices. These practices are often opaque to medical practitioners and can be harmful, especially if the patient no longer adheres to their treatment regime or experiences side-effects from herbal remedies. Illness narratives help locate some of the various alternative therapies available in Singapore and South East Asia and identify some of the reasons why patients become estranged from scientific medicine.

Teratologies and the meaning of cancer

In *Teratologies*, Jackie Stacey notes that a 'teratoma' is a particularly virulent yet treatable tumour (the word *teras* from the Greek refers to 'monster' or 'marvel' or 'portent'). Teratologies are 'the tales of monsters and marvels that pervade the cultural imaginary of cancer subcultures'.[7] Cancer narratives are typically composed of stories of diagnosis, treatment, prognosis, and survival, and yet, due to the uncertainties of treatment, to the mortality rate, and the threat of recurrence, they tend to resist closure. However, Stacey found that medical accounts of teratoma are given to exemplify the success of medical science, placing it in the role of the rescuer. Scientific knowledge is presented as ever expanding and doctors appear as heroes in the battleground between 'good science and bad disease'.[8] Meanwhile, the patient is relegated to a passive object. Conversely, in pathographies, the patient can become the hero in an archetypal tale that Frank identifies as the quest narrative.[9] Here the experience of illness is presented as a journey structured around a departure, which may be a symptom such as a lump, dizziness or a persistent cough, followed by initiation as the patient self-consciously enters into the work of recovery, and concludes with a return, in which the patient is no longer ill but has developed new knowledge from his or her trials. In the quest narrative, the ill person reorders and structures his or her experiences in a form which is often presented as a search for acceptance of illness and an attempt to find meaning in suffering. The stories that we tell about illness are culturally significant for enriching our understanding of health and sickness but they also contribute to the wider narratives in society, which in turn impact health literacy and knowledge in the population.

Medical practitioners prefer individuals to play an active role in managing their health – prevention is better than cure – and see a firm correlation between health literacy and a healthy population. Access to knowledge is facilitated or hindered by socio-cultural and economic factors and this severely impacts upon the decisions that patients make. Local contexts significantly shape the ways in which people think and talk about cancer and socio-cultural differences can and do limit the efficacy of Western-based approaches. For instance, in a recent ethnographic study of breast cancer in Singapore, the researchers were struck by the low breast cancer knowledge found in a country that possesses state-of-the-art medical services: 'As incidence rates of breast cancer escalate in Singapore, it becomes imperative to understand what factors might influence women's decisions to seek early diagnosis and treatment of the disease.'[10] Their chief concern related to the social and cultural contexts of women's daily lives in Singapore which impinge upon their ability to recognize the symptoms of breast cancer and seek medical help. Limited breast cancer knowledge has a direct impact on mortality rates and results in thousands more women dying largely due to late presentation.

Desire for information and the confidence to access it is often a privilege of those with greater educational opportunities and financial resources. Medical information is often implicitly targeted at a Western demographic and the seeming neutrality of a medical textbook houses cultural biases and naturalizes a particular type of patient. Public health campaigns are necessarily directed at a large cross-section of the population and lack the specificity and immersion that narrative can bring. Consequently, cancer narratives written by patients in Singapore can play a vital role in spreading knowledge and awareness. The next section of this essay analyses three Singaporean breast cancer narratives – Grace Segran's *Cheers to Life!* (2000), Theresa Tan's *A Clean Breast* (2013), and Charmaine Chan's *The Magic Circle* (2017). Each of them offers insight into the factors that might influence a patient's decision to seek early diagnosis; helps to explicate the procedures that a patient with cancer may expect to encounter; and highlights the impact of a cancer diagnosis on family members. I then examine pathographies written by doctors – Low Chee Kwang's *Victory over Cancer* (2010) and Ang Peng Tiam's *Doctor, I Have Cancer. Can You Help Me?* (2006). These narratives bring together phenomenological and biomedical perspectives on cancer, debunk the notion that cancer is a death sentence, and offer insight into the reasons why patients turn to alternative therapies.

Cancer Narratives in Singapore

Grace Segran is a former staff nurse who was diagnosed with breast cancer in 1998. She was forty-one years old and was on the point of moving with her husband to Jakarta for a job posting. *Cheers to Life!* recounts her experiences of this difficult period in precise and candid tones, identifying six key challenges that she was faced with: (i) the cancer diagnosis; (ii) the discovery that it had spread to her lymph nodes; (iii) separation from her daughter who was enrolled in school in Jakarta while, accompanied by her husband, she returned to Singapore for treatment; (iv) chemotherapy; (v) hair loss; (vi) menopause brought on by chemotherapy. Of these challenges, three are biomedical and three are socio-cultural which suggests that the clinic only engages fully with approximately half of their patients' concerns. The biomedical issues – the initial diagnosis, the six positive lymph nodes, and chemotherapy – highlight the fear and uncertainty faced by patients with cancer. For instance, Segran explains that radiotherapy is dependent on the patient's body being lined up with invisible rays but there is no confirmation that the procedure has been followed correctly with the beams accurately aligned. For if the patient moves, the rays will miss their target. Alongside the biomedical issues, the bulk of the narrative concerns the socio-cultural challenges faced by Segran and she discusses at length the impact of hair loss, her separation from her daughter, and the onset of menopause, each issue impacting negatively on her femininity. Segran's advice to other patients with breast cancer is to 'give yourself time to grieve the loss of womanhood', and to spend time with family as 'the best medicine, at this stage in your life'.[11]

Segran also sheds light on the economic challenges faced by patients with cancer and the difficulty of finding employment. She claims that, in a competitive job market, employers tend to reject candidates with existing medical conditions because they are likely, it is thought, to have diminished productivity.[12] However, as she notes, a job is not simply a means of generating income but helps to give direction and purpose; work can be fun, offers a social environment away from the home and clinical setting, and can ultimately be therapeutic. Employment is a significant aspect of social reintegration, helps restore a sense of normalcy or control, and aids the 'transition from being a patient to a survivor'.[13] Segran also seeks to undo cultural stereotypes common to older generations in Singapore: 'As Asians, we often avoid talking about some things. Feelings. Fears. Expressions of love. But we need to. It is not weak, nor is it "western". To love and to be loved are basic human needs.'[14] Although this assertion may surprise readers, behind it is the notion that among Singaporeans generally it is pragmatism and cognitive reasoning that are valorized. Freshmen medical students sometimes state that the values of humility, empathy, and care expressed by medical humanities scholars – while aspirational – cannot be 'accepted' in Singapore. In valorizing work and debunking the notion that emotional openness is unacceptable, Segran challenges cultural expectations faced by many women in Singapore.

Theresa Tan, former editor-in-chief of *ELLE* in Singapore, playwright, and mother of three, was diagnosed with ductal carcinoma in situ (DCIS) breast cancer at the age of forty-three. Although the disease was Stage Zero, Tan lost her right breast through a mastectomy. In her memoir, *A Clean Breast*, she details her thoughts and feelings throughout her diagnosis, treatment, and recovery. Although Tan uses narrative form to order events and bring coherence to her experience, she also addresses the fears and concerns patients have. In particular, she sheds light on consultation sessions in Singapore and the distress that a lack of empathy can cause. For instance, faced with the possibility of having cancer, she is caught between hoping for a clean bill of health and not daring to; dreading the loss of her job and attempting to plan and rationalize the impact of treatment on her work. However, the radiographer at the clinic where she is to undergo a mammogram screening, makes no effort to put her at ease and begins the ultrasound without saying a word. She is then ushered into the consultant's room: 'The tall, thin surgeon did not look up, did not catch my eye, did not say a word.'[15] The medical staff are unresponsive and treat Tan as an object rather than engage with her thoughts and anxieties as an individual.

Tan's experience also shows that patients are highly sensitive to terminology in ways that medical practitioners may overlook. During an early consultation, the doctor states that Tan has a 'thickening' in her breast but later the mammogram technologist refers to it as a 'mass':

My ears pricked up, alarmed. 'Mass?' She furrowed her brow and read out loud to me from the notes written by the clinic doctor I saw on Friday. The scan had to show the thickening ('possibly a mass', she corrected herself) under the nipple as clearly as possible.[16]

Whereas the technologist will see several cases each day to the point that conducting a mammogram becomes a routine task, for the patient the test results will determine their entire world. The wildly divergent degrees of importance attached to the procedure needs to be acknowledged by medical practitioners in order to help patients to overcome their fears and doubts. As Charon states, 'if only the doctor would, as a matter of routine, be prepared for the jarring, jolting, inarticulate presence of dread; if only he would be attuned to the inevitable and exorbitant terrors that illness brings'.[17] In contrast to the radiographer, the breast surgeon, is described by Tan as having 'a reassuring way of explaining what he was thinking and doing and how things work'.[18] In contrast to the radiographer, Hoe treats her as a partner whom he seeks to aid in making informed decisions about her treatment and care. Doctors in Singapore are encouraged to deliver 'patient-centred care' but Segran's and Tan's narratives both indicate that this ethic does not necessarily permeate into the more instrumental aspects of healthcare in which technology comes to the fore. The conversion of the patient into an instrumental text – the machine language of images, graphs, and numbers – quietens the patient's voice and risks detaching her hopes and concerns from the thoughts of the examining practitioner.

Tan also expresses certain conservative views that are at odds with liberal, anti-essentialist discourse but in general her perspective offers insight into the very real concerns Singaporean women have when considering surgery: 'a woman may be more than the sum of her parts, but she's got to have all of her parts'.[19] When Tan learns that, depending on the size of her tumour, her doctors will perform a mastectomy followed by immediate breast reconstruction, which will leave her without a nipple, her thoughts swiftly turn to her husband: 'What's a breast without a nipple? What would Kevin say or feel? These breasts were his as much as they were mine.'[20] While most readers may balk at Tan's assertion that her body is the property of her husband, her statement highlights the fact that breasts are not mere objects but cultural signifiers with a rich array of meanings and associations. For Tan, her breasts are integral to her status as a woman and symbolize her relationship with her husband, both sexually and emotionally. However, she learns to overcome her fear and, after recovering from the post-operative bruising and swelling, eventually comes to accept her reconstructed breast, and to recognize that her self-worth, as her relationships, are not bound up in her body image alone.

In *The Magic Circle*, Charmaine Chan intertwines her memories of her two sisters – Lorraine and Elaine – with the story of Elaine's cancer diagnosis and eventual death. In May 2005 Elaine was diagnosed with cholangiocarcinoma, or cancer of the bile duct, which is both rare and incurable. Following a pancreaticoduodenectomy or Whipple – named after the surgeon who refined the technique – and chemotherapy, Elaine passed away nine months later. As the family tragedy unfolded, Chan searched for a way to help and did so by revisiting the life the sisters shared and their invisible bond that is symbolized in the titular image of the circle. 'Memories are like living things, kept alive by sharing and talking about them, so that they can breathe, resuming shape and colour in your consciousness' – sharing memories, in Chan's view, offered succour and temporary respite from the sterile hospital walls.[21]

The Magic Circle recounts the lived experiences of a family dealing with cancer from a position outside of the clinic and the ways in which the illness exposes hidden tensions and causes unpredictable emotional turbulence. Chan underlines the extent to which the accumulation of unsolicited advice from relatives and friends contributes to the burden felt by the patient, reflects upon the subtle yet significant impact of physical touch, and debunks the notion that cancer is caused solely by lifestyle choices – Elaine, she recalls, followed an organic diet, avoided genetically modified foods, exercised regularly, and practised yoga. Chan also writes of how, in the face of a seemingly incurable disease, patients may turn to alternative medicine. She was shocked to discover that her previously rational sister was planning a visit to John of God, a faith healer or 'psychic surgeon' in Brazil, who lacked any medical qualifications yet performs physical procedures: 'There are videos of him cutting into people with unsanitised scalpels or inserting forceps up their noses.'[22] Chan remembers how extremely difficult it was to negotiate between offering encouragement and support to Elaine and being honest about her concerns. Regrettably, we do not learn about Elaine's experience in Brazil. Although Chan's honesty caused conflict, the disagreement ultimately enabled her sister to express her fears and frustrations in a manner that she found cathartic.

Chan's memoir emphasizes the impact of critical illness, not just on the patient, but on family members. After moving to Hong Kong, she finds that she is experiencing a physical reaction to grief: 'there are episodes of sudden nausea, enough to stop you in the street, enough that you double over and retch, holding on to street railings and lampposts for support'.[23] Panic attacks necessitate recourse to figurative language: 'you are suddenly gripped by a feeling like the ground has disappeared beneath your feet, like you can't breathe, like you are drowning or suffocating or both'; and at other times, the intensity of the emotional pain is such that it feels corporeal 'like someone has just punched you in the gut'.[24] As an indescribable yet implacable force, cancer is often overdetermined and Chan also calls it by many names. She considers 'Cancer' to have 'all the characteristics of an invading army – cold, faceless, efficient and merciless' that conquers the territory of her sister's body, unimpeded by reinforcements like Chemotherapy and Radiation.[25] She later names it the Beast, 'a hateful tormentor' that, first, 'devours her, gnawing on her flesh' and then 'proceeds to inflate different bits of her, just for its amusement'.[26] The Beast describes the corporeal manifestations of the illness that make the body appear manipulated and twisted in new forms. Towards the end, the cancer appears differently. 'These days, its familiarity makes it seem more like a big friendly Mastiff. No longer malign, no longer malevolent, it is nevertheless always there – a constant, unwavering, patient presence.'[27] As Elaine's illness progresses the mastiff is described as lying quietly or taking up position at the foot of the bed 'biding its time'.[28] Mastiffs are one of the largest yet also one of the shortest-lived dog breeds. Rather than an invading force or a monstrous beast, cancer has become a companion. The mastiff analogy runs against the grain of cancer narratives that typically draw on journey and battle metaphors, and instead signals acceptance of a traumatic reality. It suggests that naming a disease and using a private language help to restore a much-needed semblance of control to patients and their families in the face of a relentless terminal illness.

Illness narratives in Singapore are not only written by patients but by doctors, some of whom also become patients. Among members of the medical profession who have published cancer narratives, Ang Peng Tiam recounts stories from the clinic and offers insight into individual struggles with critical illness.[29] Meanwhile Low Chee Kwang whose work I discuss below writes about his experience with cancer of the lymphatic system and the ways in which it influenced his medical practice.

Low was born in 1961 and works as an orthopaedic surgeon in the private sector. He excelled at school but encountered difficulty passing the examination in medicine. Although he possessed the requisite knowledge to perform surgery, he lacked the communication skills necessary to inspire confidence in the patient. Widening his singular focus on technical proficiency to encompass patient care enabled him eventually to pass the examination. Whereas in the past, he had 'viewed everyone as a competitor', he learns that collaboration and empathy are integral skills in the profession.[30] He was diagnosed with cancer twice in his life: first, with Hodgkin's lymphoma in 1981 and again with diffuse large B cell non-Hodgkin's lymphoma in 2007. Robert Klitzman notes that personal experiences of illness commonly reverses the detachment that has developed through years of professional medical training: 'In facing the darkness of their own disease, these doctors often came to treat patients and to teach trainees better.'[31] Similarly, Low notes that his experience has helped stimulate greater empathy for his patients: 'Because I have been ill and have suffered, I know what they face and what they might be feeling.'[32] Consequently, he is alert to the impact of a patient's critical illness on family members, on their financial situation, and the emotions felt by patients faced with uncertain prognosis.

His first-person account of the often-invasive diagnostic procedures and treatments also discloses the hidden private concerns that patients may be harbouring including a sense of lost dignity and autonomy, of defamiliarization of the body, and of how lack of control over quotidian bodily operations such as bowel movements becomes an issue of immense concern midway through an invasive, tedious, and time-consuming diagnostic procedure. We also learn that pre-operation procedures can be more frightening than the operation itself and that harmful side-effects can appear, unrecognized by the patient. For instance, a high dose of steroids was to cause Low to develop insomnia and become restless and energetic: 'I was walking about the house in the middle of the night. I talked excessively and at a very high speed so people could not understand what I said. I shouted loudly whenever I was confronted.'[33] Anecdotes like these highlight the need for close family support and careful explanation of the potential harms involved in treatment. In his own practice, Low does not simply list possible complications but stresses that the chances of these complications occurring can be minimized by taking appropriate precautions. Hence, patients are empowered to play a role, albeit a minor one, in their treatment. 'I like to return to them some sense of control because when they find themselves subjected to a whole range of treatments that are new to them, it can be traumatic.'[34]

Whereas patient-authored cancer narratives tend to conclude with remission and messages of hope, Ang draws on his experience as an oncologist to offer insight into a wide range of cases, many of which serve as cautionary tales about the perils of late diagnosis. He details the experience of a patient with locally advanced breast cancer who waited eight months before seeking treatment. Her husband had been undergoing treatment for incurable stage IV stomach cancer and when Ang asked why she delayed, she replied: 'I didn't want to deal with it, because I felt that my husband's life was more important.'[35] Although tempted to attribute this statement to denial, Ang reasons that she was concerned about the cost of her treatment. Ang also reports on a patient who saw a faith healer before coming to the clinic; this caused a delay which resulted in the cancer growing and breaking through the skin. Finally, he gives a more extreme example of denial, the results of which are detailed in graphic terms. This patient had suffered for months without seeing a doctor:

> She had known of the lump months ago but did not want to tell her husband. She hid herself whenever she bathed so that he would not see it. When the lump became an open sore and started to smell, she doused herself with perfume.[36]

Her husband and son had to trick her into visiting the doctor and, when asked by Ang why she had delayed so long, she responded: 'I am *very* scared of surgery.'[37] Denialism is a constant among cancer patients to varying degrees and Ang's narratives indicate that non-acceptance is a major cause of treatment delays, which can result in the condition becoming incurable. Illness narratives can help doctors anticipate – and understand the reasons behind – denialism, and they may also help sufferers to consider seeking early diagnosis and adhere to treatment regimes.

Despite popular belief, modern medicine is not a positivist Newtonian science. As Brody points out, 'medicine has grown and evolved over centuries as an integrated and unified practice' that requires the ability to interpret a vast array of signs and symptoms found in individual patients.[38] In the 1940s the historian, Erwin H. Ackerknecht, reminded practitioners that medicine is an art that differs from pure sciences by virtue of its focus on 'patients, that is, whole human beings, not disordered metabolisms, specific infections, or neoplasms'.[39] Although practitioners draw on generalizable scientific knowledge, clinical judgment is always particular and experiential. The widespread misdescription of medicine as a science means that patients typically expect certainty from their physicians. However, as Kathryn Montgomery notes, 'medicine will never know everything for every case, and the knowledge physicians have will not always translate into effective action'.[40] Trust in medical practitioners inevitably demands acceptance of uncertainty. Although patients are typically given access to the statistical uncertainties of treatment and prognosis, perception of the data is subjective and dependent upon the guidance of the attending physician. Consequently, trust and communication between doctors and patients is necessary for effective treatment.

Conclusion

The word 'pathography' has undergone a dramatic semantic shift from being an account or description of a disease written by a physician observing a patient to become the primary means by which a patient's lived experience and voice are restored to the medical encounter. Unlike other, more instrumental discourses, illness narratives express the uncertainties and ambiguities of being ill, extend our understanding beyond biological perspectives, and challenge the misdescription of medicine as a positivist science. As Montgomery points out, the 'everyday understanding of physicians' work is still lodged in descriptions that are crude, incomplete, and unreflective'.[41] Such descriptions suggest that medicine can offer certainty in the face of disease and imply that doctors can successfully repress their emotional responses to sickness. The problem with this approach is that, while doctors will be affected too by their emotions, they will be unable to exercise clinical judgement effectively if they are not conscious of them. Whereas clinical case reports seek to simplify and contain indeterminacy, illness narratives in Singapore expose the fears and concerns that patients face. Whereas oncologists typically consider the statistical odds of recovery and life expectancy, the success or failure of the treatment will determine the patient's entire world.

   The discourse of uncertainty and risk suffuses all of the cancer narratives discussed above. Segran's description of biomedical procedures focuses on her lack of agency and the necessarily uncertain outcomes. By contrast, socio-cultural issues are depicted as opportunities for renewal and personal growth. Meanwhile, when Tan's technologist talks about a mass rather than a thickening or her surgeon refuses to engage in eye contact or discuss her condition, they introduce an additional unwarranted level of uncertainty to the medical encounter. Similarly, when Chan's sister seeks out a 'psychic surgeon' in Brazil, she does so in search of certainty in the face of implacable odds. Consequently, Chan's metaphor of cancer as a mastiff, 'a constant, unwavering, patient presence', helps, as I have suggested, to alleviate her feelings of uncertainty.[42] Low's experience with cancer has attuned him to the uncertainty experienced by patients and consequently he seeks to inform his own patients about their condition and to attempt to restore their agency. Finally, Ang details how fear, uncertainty, and denial can lead patients to delay treatment or seek alternative therapies that can lead to unnecessary complications. Illness narratives comprise a powerful mode of expression because they do not reduce or seek to contain the risk, doubt, and fear that patients feel. Instead they present an ontology of uncertainty that expands the horizons of instrumental medical discourse from an exclusive focus on the disease to restore the human being to the centre of the medical encounter.

NOTES

1. Anne Hunsaker Hawkins, *Reconstructing Illness: Studies in Pathography*, 2nd edn (West Lafayette, Indiana: Purdue UP, 1999), p. 3. Lisa Diedrich, *Treatments: Language, Politics, and the Culture of Illness* (Minneapolis and London: U of Minnesota P, 2007), p. xvii.
2. Arthur Frank, *The Wounded Storyteller: Body, Illness, and Ethics* (Chicago: U of Chicago P, 1997). Arthur Kleinman, *The Illness Narratives* (New York: Basic Books, 1988). Howard Brody, *Stories of Sickness* (Oxford: Oxford UP, 2003).
3. Stella Bolaki, *Illness as Many Narratives: Arts, Medicine, and Culture* (Edinburgh: Edinburgh UP, 2017).
4. Nicole M. Piemonte, *Afflicted: How Vulnerability Can Heal Medical Education and Practice* (Cambridge, Mass.: MIT Press, 2018), p. 37.
5. Frank, *The Wounded Storyteller*, p. 6.
6. Hawkins, *Reconstructing Illness*, p. 4.
7. Jackie Stacey, *Teratologies: A Cultural Study of Cancer* (London: Routledge, 1997), p. 10.
8. Stacey, *Teratologies*, p. 11.
9. Frank, *The Wounded Storyteller*, pp. 115-36.
10. Celene Wei Qi Ng, Miriam Koktvedgaard Zeitzen, and Cynthia Chou, 'Breast Cancer Journeys in Singapore', in *Breast Cancer Meanings: Journeys Across Asia*, eds, Cynthia Chou and Miriam Koktvedgaard Zeitzen (Singapore: NUS Press, 2018), pp. 136-7.
11. Grace Segran, *Cheers to Life! One Woman's Dance with Breast Cancer* (Self-published, 2000), p. 56.
12. A recent report suggests that the strongest factors related to intention to hire were 'the employer's efficacy, followed by the employer's attitude towards cancer survivors. The strongest factor related to intention to retain was perceived moral obligations, followed by attitude toward cancer, and employment situation'. Angela Ka Ying Mak, Shirley S. Ho, and Hyo Jung Kim, 'Factors Related to Employers' Intent to Hire, Retain and Accommodate Cancer Survivors: The Singapore Perspective', *Journal of Occupational Rehabilitation*, 24 (2014) 725-31, p. 730.
13. Z. Amir, D. Neary, and K. Luker, 'Cancer Survivors' Views of Work 3 Years Post Diagnosis: A UK Perspective', *European Journal of Oncological Nursing*, 12 (2008) 190-7.
14. Segran, *Cheers to Life!*, p. 106.
15. Theresa Tan, *A Clean Breast* (Singapore: Write Editions, 2013), p. 25.
16. Tan, *A Clean Breast*, p. 21.
17. Rita Charon, *Narrative Medicine: Honoring the Stories of Sickness* (Oxford: Oxford UP, 2006), p. 20.
18. Tan, *A Clean Breast*, p. 30.
19. Tan, *A Clean Breast*, p. 49.
20. Tan, *A Clean Breast*, p. 40.

21. Charmaine Chan, *The Magic Circle* (Singapore: Ethos, 2017), p. 16.
22. Chan, *The Magic Circle*, p. 79.
23. Chan, *The Magic Circle*, p. 108.
24. Chan, *The Magic Circle*, p. 108.
25. Chan, *The Magic Circle*, p. 237.
26. Chan, *The Magic Circle*, pp. 237-8.
27. Chan, *The Magic Circle*, p. 238.
28. Chan, *The Magic Circle*, p. 251.
29. Ang Peng Tiam, *Doctor, I Have Cancer. Can You Help Me? A Book of Hope. True Stories from the Cancer Clinic* (Singapore: SNP International, 2006).
30. Low Chee Kwang, *Victory over Cancer: God is Gracious* (Singapore: Armour, 2010), p. 33.
31. Robert Klitzman, *When Doctors Become Patients* (Oxford: Oxford UP, 2008), p. 257.
32. Low, *Victory over Cancer*, p. 54.
33. Low, *Victory over Cancer*, p. 48.
34. Low, *Victory over Cancer*, p. 55.
35. Ang, *Doctor*, p. 48.
36. Ang, *Doctor*, p. 54.
37. Ang, *Doctor*, p. 54.
38. Brody, *Stories of Sickness*, p. 51.
39. Erwin H. Ackerknecht, 'The Role of Medical History in Medical Education', *Bulletin of the History of Medicine*, 21:2 (1947) 135-45, p. 144.
40. Kathryn Montgomery, *How Doctors Think: Clinical Judgment and the Practice of Medicine* (Oxford: Oxford UP, 2006), p. 27.
41. Montgomery, *How Doctors Think*, p. 30.
42. Chan, *The Magic Circle*, p. 238.

On the Back of a Hyena: Depression and the (Post-)Colonial Context in Tsitsi Dangarembga's *This Mournable Body*

AMY RUSHTON

Reading for mental distress in Tsitsi Dangarembga's classic novel, *Nervous Conditions* (1988), is well-trodden territory, particularly focused, as it has been, upon Nyasha's disordered eating.[1] Clare Barker reminds us that multiple 'nervous conditions' are evident throughout the narrative, complicating 'diagnostic boundaries between the normal and the pathological', and encouraging 'critique of the processes by which healthy bodies and psyches are rendered unhealthy and endangered'.[2] To date, however, relatively little attention has been paid to the depressive, dissociative tone and behaviour of Tambu, the narrator-protagonist of *Nervous Conditions* and its two sequels, *The Book of Not* (2006) and the recently published *This Mournable Body* (2018).[3] Yet it is Tambu who controls the narrative in all three novels, a narrator who, as Dangarembga stated in 2004, 'may not have been psychologically contorted when she was fourteen [but] definitely is now'.[4] In this article, I argue that *This Mournable Body* unleashes a specific mental distress that has been building within Tambu since *Nervous Conditions*: a severe, chronic depression cultivated by ongoing colonial oppression within 'free' Zimbabwe and its intersecting racial, gender, and economic inequalities.

In exploring the disruptive potential of mental distress in *This Mournable Body*, I find that Frantz Fanon proves to be a productive corollary. This is not surprising perhaps given that it has long been common practice to discuss Dangarembga's work in dialogue with Fanon. The title, *Nervous Conditions*, after all, is inspired by the English translation of Jean Paul Sartre's controversial preface to *The Wretched of the Earth*.[5] More significantly, the recent publication of Fanon's previously inaccessible remaining work – speeches and lectures, alongside plays and academic papers – further strengthens and adds new dimensions to the epistemic bonds between these two canonical writers. In *The Wretched of the Earth*, Fanon observes that 'successful colonization' is characterized by 'a regular and important mental pathology which is the direct product of oppression'.[6] Note that this pathology is not characterized by fear but by a kind of calm; for Fanon, successful colonization prevails over a *subdued* community. In postcolonial studies – particularly in the humanities – we tend to, understandably, focus on the traumatic effect that life under colonialism inflicts upon subjectivity. Yet it strikes me that Fanon's work draws attention to the subterranean disquiet and distress that takes a psychological toll. When Fanon speaks of the warped 'consistence, coherence and homogeneity' established within the colonized world and how oppression 'depersonalizes' the individual, it is difficult to ignore the parallels with the *long durée* of chronic depression's banal, often dissociative experiences.[7] As Ann Cvetkovich observes, the typical characteristics of depression – silence, weariness, and numbness – are *perfect* conditions for the perpetuation of oppression.[8] Depression is not only an 'affective register' of societal discontent but also 'one that often keeps people [from] really noticing the sources of their unhappiness'.[9] Contemporary depressive subjects struggle to see the reasons for their unhappiness or distress beyond themselves; messages reinforced by a neoliberal society and bio-psychiatric model tell us that the fault lies within us and not to look beyond ourselves. Cvetkovich is referring specifically here to a contemporary North American context, but the parallels between depression in a neoliberal capitalist world and the twentieth-century colonial context are not only striking but, I would argue, part of the same historical lineage.

Of course, there are inevitable problems when referring to depression in a colonial context. Writing at a time of ongoing colonization across Africa, Fanon reminds us that colonialism is not only concerned with political, geographic, cultural and ideological domination but also *psychological* domination. For Fanon, if the aim of psychiatry is to reconcile patient to situation, then this is impossible in a racist society, absurd in the colonial context, and undesirable for a decolonizing society. There is a twin violence at work: the Eurocentric origins of the psychiatry transported to the majority world, and the impossible conditions for recovery, which usually means conforming to white, European logics of 'success'. China Mills, for example, has urgently drawn attention to the contemporary construction of depression among other mental 'illnesses', and to how psychiatry, 'a colonial legacy in many parts of the global South', has served to propagate 'new and continued forms of oppression' by controlling subjects via diagnosis and treatment.[10] My intention here is not to diagnose or read for depression in *This Mournable Body*; I contend that Dangarembga's third novel mediates depressive states-of-mind as an *affective* psychological and physical exploration of a violently oppressive colonial – and postcolonial – world. Tambu's increasingly depersonalized narration is reminiscent of Fanon's observations of the alienated and dissociative psychological condition of the colonized subject – particularly by the third novel.

Who are 'you'? Tambu's progress

Published across a thirty-year period, *Nervous Conditions, The Book of Not*, and *This Mournable Body* document the life of Tambu from adolescence to middle age. Considered a classic of postcolonial fiction and one of the most widely taught Anglophone African texts, Dangarembga's first novel follows Tambu from her home in a rural homestead in Rhodesia to her uncle's home, where she is permitted to be educated after her elder brother unexpectedly dies. Although desperate for further education, Tambu finds that the opportunity brings neither peace nor satisfaction. Her disquiet is further emphasized by her cousin and agemate, Nyasha, who is quick to point out the hypocrisies and contradictions of social advancement in a colonized world. The sequel, *The Book of Not*, picks up where *Nervous Conditions* leaves Tambu: at a Catholic boarding school, where Tambu finds herself in a tiny minority of black students. Unlike the first novel, *The Book of Not* sees the political realm creeping into Tambu's world as the fight for independence impacts the school girls. After a promising early academic career, Tambu's determination is steadily crushed by the injustices inflicted upon her, such as being denied the school prize in favour of a less-deserving white student and, in her career in an advertising agency, when her work is credited to a white male colleague. *The Book of Not* ends with Rhodesia becoming Zimbabwe and Tambu finding that her supposedly post-independence world does not offer the opportunities she expected.

This Mournable Body confirms suspicions that things are not well with Tambu. Once again, it begins immediately after the previous novel's events. Tambu is unemployed, having resigned from her copywriting job, and in need of cheaper accommodation. Her distress spirals in a world where her blackness and femaleness are further undermined by the restricted opportunities for employment and advancement in Zimbabwe. Oscillating between, on the one hand, extremes of anger and enjoying witnessing (and then perpetrating) violence inflicted on young women and, on the other, retreating to her bed and tangled thoughts, Tambu has concerns that she 'will start thinking of ending it all'.[11] Instead, she endures a mental and emotional collapse that leads to her being admitted into hospital care and then released under the supervision of Nyasha, who has returned from Germany with a husband and children in tow.

The changes in Tambu's psychological character are emphasized in *This Mournable Body*'s choice of narrative perspective: the first person 'I' narration of *Nervous Conditions* and *The Book of Not* shifts to the second person 'you', thus implicating the reader in Tambu's thoughts and behaviour. This narrative shift not only heightens Tambu's dissociative state of mind but also circles back to the first book. As we know, the title, *Nervous Conditions*, is derived from a section of Sartre's controversial preface. In the preface, Sartre argues why Fanon's work is important for a European readership by attempting to convey the viewpoint of the oppressed 'natives' under colonial rule:

> Europeans, ... Fanon explains you to his brothers ... If I were them, you may say, I'd prefer my mumbo-jumbo to their Acropolis ... [Y]ou've grasped the situation. But not altogether, because you *aren't* them – or not yet. Otherwise you would know that they can't choose; they must have both. Two worlds ... they dance all night and at dawn they crowd into the churches to hear mass; each day the split widens. Our enemy betrays his brothers and becomes our accomplice; his brothers do the same thing. The status of 'native' is a nervous condition introduced and maintained by the settler among colonized people *with their consent*.[12]

While the binary distinction between 'colonizer' and 'native' is, rightfully, more complex in Dangarembga's trilogy, Sartre's troubling assertion that the 'nervous condition' of the colonized subject is *consensual* provides an important lens through which to view Tambu.[13] Caught up in a world shaped by white supremacy, capitalism, and patriarchy, Tambu's anxiety is fuelled by the impossibility of equilibrium: as the trilogy continues, Tambu's mental distress unravels as she confronts the reality of the colonized and then post-independence world she lives in. No matter how hard she strives, Tambu's being black, female, and African forms multiple barriers to her access to education, money, and status. Tambu's willing attempt to succeed in an inequal and unjust society dooms her to psychological collapse.

Aside from the notion of anxiety as a key component of colonial oppression, Sartre's preface mirrors a crucial formal shift in *This Mournable Body*: in his insistence on addressing the reader as 'you', Sartre attempts to bridge a gap of experiential understanding but, instead, perpetuates the othering distance between the presumed European reader and the silent African subject by reinforcing the oppositional binary.[14] However, Tambu's subdued presence and, later, dissociative voice in her own narratives allows

Dangarembga to reappropriate the othering, dissociative perspective created in Sartre's preface. Compare the opening lines, first, from *Nervous Conditions* and, second, from *This Mournable Body*:

> I was not sorry when my brother died. Nor am I apologising for my callousness, as you may define it, my lack of feeling. For it is not that at all. I feel many things these days, much more than I was able to feel in the days when I was young and my brother died ...[15]

> There is a fish in the mirror. The mirror is above the washbasin in the corner of your hostel room. Still in bed, you roll onto your back and stare at the ceiling. Realizing your arm has gone to sleep, you move it back and forth with your working hand until pain bursts through in a blitz of pins and needles.[16]

The direct, assertive retrospective narrative has now been replaced by an irreal, dissociative perspective, a narrative process that began in *The Book of Not*: the second novel opens with an ablated leg arcing through the air before landing in a tree, the circumstances of the image being unclear and surreal.[17] The limb, in fact, belongs to Netsai, Tambu's younger sister and a guerrilla soldier in the war of independence. Tambu is witnessing her sister's lifechanging, and near-fatal, injury caused by Netsai's stepping on a live explosive as she heads back into the bush from their village. By *This Mournable Body*, Tambu does not even seem to be controlling the narrative perspective in the novel's opening lines: after the first-person accounts of *Nervous Conditions* and *The Book of Not*, it is jarring to no longer be 'hearing' from Tambu but to be embodying her – especially during such a tumultuous and disconcerting narrative.

Although *This Mournable Body* marks a shift in the intensity and narration of Tambu's mental distress, her seemingly depressive behaviour is consistent across the trilogy. There are clues in *Nervous Conditions* and *The Book of Not* that Tambu is undergoing mental distress, although the more explicit incidences are observed by her in other characters.[18] Tambu's own distress is largely characterized by lethargy and stasis – which does not make for the most dynamic action. One of the reasons I think the depressive quality of Tambu has not been subject to critical scrutiny is that depression is, frankly, not very exciting nor dramatic. Furthermore, the representation and interpretation of depression is also, arguably, less legible within the critical frameworks most frequently applied to *Nervous Conditions* and *The Book of Not*. It follows then that Nyasha's explicit hybridity and self-professed cultural conflicts are more straightforward to analyse alongside established ideas associated with postcolonial criticism: Tambu's cousin readily articulates her own 'nervous conditions' within the first novel and the reader is able to satisfactorily 'diagnose' her various disorders. Such a reading strategy is not inherently misguided: indeed, the theoretically referential quality of Nyasha's distress is one reason why *Nervous Conditions* endures as a useful and popular text for teaching. However, Tambu's own turmoil is equally significant, albeit more slippery in its meaning – and necessarily so.

As previously stated, my intention is not to 'diagnose' Tambu as a chronic depressive; rather, I am exploring the potential of depression as a critique of colonialism and its legacies, as opposed to, say, a reading that prioritizes traumatic theories. Throughout *Nervous Conditions*, Tambu's own inner turmoil is heightened whenever she cannot occupy herself: 'there were things I was not supposed to be thinking of, and the thoughts would creep back in ... leaving me anxious and sleepless without knowing exactly why'.[19] By *This Mournable Body*, Tambu becomes increasingly weary, her time devoted to supressing 'feelings of doom' while sitting on her bed, staring out of the window.[20]

As Cvetkovich suggests, depression is frequently characterized as a sense of impasse, of feeling 'stuck', and 'that things will not move forward due to circumstance – not that they can't, but that the world is not designed to make it happen or there has been a failure of imagination'.[21] The slowing of moments and lethargy associated with the depressed body appear to be a consequence of the stasis of the depressed mind. I do not mean that the mind is inactive; rather, that the depressed person cannot psychologically nor physically move beyond their present.

The sense of impasse with depression is important because physical stasis is a key part of colonial control, a symptom of the banality of everyday violence. In *The Wretched of the Earth*, Fanon conveys the lived experience of the colonized subject – the alienation from self and community – by presenting the colonial world as one in which the 'native is a being hemmed in':

> The first thing which the native learns is to stay in his place, and not to go beyond certain limits. This is why the dreams of the native are always of muscular prowess; his dreams are of action and of aggression.[22]

Here, Fanon makes clear the relationship between the somatic empowerment of physical and psychological freedom and the pervasive, insidious effects of living in a colonized environment, particularly the segregated settler colonies of Algeria and Zimbabwe. The restrictive, controlled environment of the colonial world provides the perfect conditions for the mind to experience a failure of imagination, denying even a discernible glimmer of liberation on the horizon. Depression is a logical response to the colonial world's deep, unjust entrenchment of inequality.

Of ants and *Njuzu*: Dissociation

The lethargy and stasis associated with depression do not have to mean passive acceptance of the colonial status quo. In *Nervous Conditions*, young Tambu's one moment of rebellion against her benefactor uncle is in her refusal to leave her bed and attend the legal wedding ceremony he enforces on her parents, an event which causes her deep shame at her parents being forced to submit to a public act that, essentially, confirms Tambu's hitherto 'illegitimacy' and feels like a mockery of her immediate family.[23]

Tambu's lethargy becomes a recurring pattern from *The Book of Not* onwards: however, her dissociation of consciousness and bodily self in *The Book of Not* and *This Mournable Body* is no longer an act of rebellion against others but rather a form of self-harm. Tambu finds herself unable to sustain her younger self's levels of ambition and motivation in the face of her increasing exposure to racism in a society built upon white supremacy. In *The Book of Not*, her comprehension of the racism restricting her social progress is not fully realized. By the time of *This Mournable Body*, she is able to identify her time at the Catholic boarding school as the defining moment of her 'metamorphosis' from the determined young girl of *Nervous Conditions* to this ground-down, subdued woman of the present:

> how awful it is to admit that closeness to white people at the convent had ruined your heart, had caused your womb, from which you reproduced yourself before you gave birth to anything else, to shrink between your hip bones.[24]

Not only does confrontation with the colonial world lead to a 'failure of imagination' for Tambu, it also produces a failure of self-creation, of identify formation. The womb, a space of creation, becomes a space of failure.

Tambu's sense of alienation from herself and others is heightened by her mental and emotional states taking the form of ants, hyenas, fish and snakes. As she unpicks her memories of encountering and taking on the lessons of white supremacy, Tambu is increasingly beset by ants crawling around and over her. Whenever ants appear in *This Mournable Body*, it is never clear to Tambu nor the reader if the ants are material or imagined. What *is* apparent is that ants are symbolic of Tambu's uncomfortable, intrusive thoughts; even her thoughts are removed from her, depersonalized and manifested as swarming insects. When she wakes up on the street, hungover from a night out with Christine, the niece of her landlady and a former comrade of Netsai's from the liberation struggle, Tambu notices '[a]nts and tiny spiders' scurrying around her 'in indignation', before 'trek[king] over [her] body'.[25] Due to her actually lying on the ground, outside, it is possible that these insects exist; however, as her hungover, exhausted state allows her critical and self-loathing thoughts to occupy her mind, Tambu continues to find the insects on her body and starts to see the ants within her lodgings.[26] As '[t]he ants file with you, past you, and into you',

> [y]ou panic at this symptom that persists into relative sobriety. ... In dread you traverse your room. Even as you lower yourself onto your bed, you know it is not your intention to engage with the things that must be faced. The insects advance up the bed's legs and into the covers the moment you thud onto the mattress.[27]

Even her own emotions and thoughts appear to be separated from her inner and bodily selves. At Nyasha's home following her breakdown, Tambu notices her uncle's old desk, and is prompted into self-reflection, struggling to fathom why, unlike herself, 'Nyasha's peculiarities do not prevent her from achieving'.[28] As Tambu reflects, she sees an ant running across the desk, and is 'suspicious that it has crawled out of [her] imagination' due to the insect being symbolic of her intrusive thoughts. Checking, she closes and opens her eyes, and finding 'it is still there, on urgent business', decides that she 'will be like the ant': 'You do not yet know how, but come what may, you will focus on the prize until you possess it.'[29] Tambu here attempts to change the significance of the ant: rather than being a manifestation of her own reeling narrative and alienated self, she chooses to interpret the ant as symbolic of industriousness and single-minded determination. Her young self, essentially. This interpretation does not last long: a few pages later, Tambu squashes an ant which leaves no physical trace on her finger.[30] Even before the symbol of her rediscovered determination can be fully realized, she unthinkingly obliterates it.

Ants are only one of a few animals associated with Tambu's dissociative, depressive state. Although Tambu's distress shares the recognizable characteristics of what is frequently recognized as depression, *This Mournable Body* adds further contextual layers to her experience. In other words, Tambu's depression is reminiscent of conditions diagnosed and 'treated' by European psychiatric discourse, yet there are also connections to existing, culturally specific ideas of (un)wellbeing due to spiritual interference. In the novel's opening, it is possible to read the 'fish in the mirror' as a hallucination, thus heightening Tambu's dissociative sense of self: 'the fish stares back at you out of purplish eye sockets, its mouth gaping, cheeks drooping as though under the weight of monstrous scales. You cannot look at yourself'.[31] The uncanny appearance of the fish that is both Tambu and not Tambu is reminiscent of the *njuzu* in Shona mythology (the Shona being Tambu's people), 'a water spirit which sometimes has human head, arms, and torso and a fish tail', 'usually pale in complexion with long, straight hair'.[32] The *njuzu* features in another classic Zimbabwean literary text, Dambudzo Marechera's *The House of Hunger* (1978), where Marechera names the spirit 'manfish' due to its human-like appearance.[33] Although the *njuzu* is 'usually an ambivalent figure, with a capacity for extremes of good and evil', Marechera's manfish is 'an evil, disruptive creature'.[34] At its most threatening, the *njuzu* is known to 'inhabit deep pools and seize children', destroying families.[35] Most significantly, Grant Lilford suggests that, in Shona literature, the *njuzu* functions as a 'catalyst' for 'social disorder and conflict ... underscoring and exacerbating existing conflicts'.[36] As *This Mournable Body* opens, Tambu recognizes the *njuzu* in the mirror as being both herself and yet *not* herself:

> You pad away from the washbasin to pull your wardrobe door open. The fish bloats to the size of a hippopotamus in the oily white paint that covers the wardrobe's wooden panelling. You turn away, not wanting to see the lumbering shadow that is your reflection.[37]

At the beginning of the novel, Tambu-as-*njuzu* overwhelms her sense of self and, as in Marechera's *The House of Hunger*, the *njuzu* signifies disruption. Tambu-as-*njuzu* foreshadows the disruption to come: chiefly, the violence she inflicts upon herself and others.

Riding hyenas: Violence

Alongside ants and the *njuzu*, Tambu's depression is characterized by a further non-human counterpart, one that also has connections to Shona lore. Like the ants and *njuza*, the hyena is a complex manifestation of distress that is both bound up with Tambu's sense of self and yet also threatens to destroy her. In *This Mournable Body*, the hyena's laugh becomes a terrifying sign of Tambu's distress at its peak, erupting when her sanity threatens to break apart completely. In the second part of the novel, Tambu awakens in the psychiatric ward of a hospital with the following thoughts:

> Now you understand. *You arrived on the back of a hyena.* The treacherous creature dropped you from far above onto a desert floor ... *You are an ill-made person. You are being*

unmade. The hyena laugh-howls at your destruction. It screams like a demented spirit and the floor dissolves beneath you.[38]

Hyenas have significance in southern African folklore as witches' familiars; David Lan explains that witches travel at night, 'rid[ing] on the backs of hyenas'.[39] A person may become a witch by being 'involuntarily possessed by the *shave*, or non-human spirit, of the hyena'.[40] Tambu's statement that she 'arrived on the back of a hyena' implies that she recognizes something of the witch about her condition, yet the hyena is also 'treacherous' as it has dropped her wilfully. The ambivalence of the hyena's significance to her condition denies Tambu, and the reader, a straightforward reason behind her distress: the hyena's agency – as suggested by treachery – suggests that witchcraft cannot be the sole reason for her distress.

That Tambu sees her interior and exterior selves as external creatures suggests that she understands herself as barely human, barely a person. In the midst of her psychological ordeal, she claims that she is simultaneously 'an ill-made person ... being unmade', a never fully formed person who is now unravelling even further.[41] In her view, along with a family, an education, and a society that has failed her, Tambu is confronted with the realization that she has somehow failed to 'make' herself into a useful and productive person. Without the perception of success or illusion of possible attainment, the little sense of self she possesses further dissolves. The hyena laughs because it already knows that Tambu cannot succeed in a world that is designed to obstruct the social advancement of a young black woman. The hyena knows because the hyena *is* Tambu: '[t]hey do not know what it is to struggle with the prospect that the hyena is you, nor how this combat marshals in the task of finishing the brutish animal off, while ensuring you remain alive yourself'.[42] From experience, the frightening aspect of severe depression is one's awareness that, even during bad episodes, extreme self-loathing thoughts are both out of our control and yet emanating from us. Even when we can recognize in the moment that internal criticisms are plainly false or a warped version of a truth, in the same moment such falsehoods and half-truths still convince us. Severe depression is parasitical and contradictory:

> You feel you are creeping over the edge of a precipice and that this cliff beckons you; worse, that you have a secret desire to fall over its edge into oblivion and that there is no way to stop that fall because *you are the precipice.*[43]

Tambu's experience captures the paradoxical, entangled nature of acute distress. She is scared of the hyena, yet she *is* the hyena, just like she cannot stop her fall because she *is* the precipice, barely separating herself from oblivion. In this section of the novel, Tambu is simultaneously victim and perpetrator.

Tambu's connection to the disruptive *njuzu* eand the 'brutish' hyena emphasizes how the assumed characteristics of depression may manifest themselves in specific culturally situated ways in oppressive contexts. Indeed, in Tambu's world, the violence of the everyday produces a different kind of violence associated with psychological distress. Rather than the self-violence or suicidal ideation more readily associated with depression or melancholia, Tambu projects her anger onto the world, eventually lashing out with disastrous consequences. Tambu's psychological distress erupts as violence against others, rather than the self. In *This Mournable Body*, her decisive mental 'break' begins with her beating a school pupil about the head, so severely that she causes the girl to become deaf in one ear.[44] That the target of her rage is a young woman is significant, both in relation to her entanglement with the hyena *shave* and the *njuzu*, and how this circles back to Tambu's story across the three novels. A person can be transformed into a witch by being possessed by the *shave* of a hyena, and in Shona lore, '[w]itches kill people, including their own children'.[45] Similarly, the *njuzu* are associated with the stealing of children, as aforementioned.[46] Lan suggests that in the case of witches, '[e]nvy is the motive most commonly ascribed, either envy of the rich by the poor or of the fertile by the barren'.[47] Throughout the trilogy, Tambu's envy of others is a recurring trait: she envies her elder brother, her cousin Nyasha, her classmates at Sacred Heart – particularly Tracey, who then ends up as her colleague and eventual employer. Whereas envy helped to drive her previous sense of ambition, by the conclusion of *The Book of Not* Tambu understands that her efforts bring her no closer to the economic and professional success she craves. In *This Mournable Body*, her disappointments have no outlet except to sink her into resentment with the 'question of who can and cannot, who does or does not succeed, return[ing] to echo ominously ... Once more, you hear the hyena laughing as you drift off to sleep'.[48] Tambu's envy, along with her self-loathing, transforms into an anger that will lead to violence.

The correspondences underlined between Tambu's psychological state and the political situation in Zimbabwe are significant. Events in *The Book of Not* appear to promise a new dawn, and the alleviation of the gendered and racial injustice of the colonial world. Yet the eruptions of overt violence in the second novel are directly linked to Zimbabwe's anticolonial moment: Netsai losing her leg, the parental deaths of (white) schoolmates, and Babamakuru's spinal injury due to a stray bullet during independence celebrations. This does not surprise since we know from Fanon's work that the colonial world is one defined by violence. However, Fanon's understanding of violence is much more nuanced: violence is banal, commonplace, normalized. As he points out,

> The colonial regime is a regime instituted by violence. ... But the violence ... is not only a violence perceived by the spirit, it is also a violence manifested in the daily behaviour of the colonized towards the colonized: *apartheid* in South Africa [etc]. ... Colonialism, however, is not satisfied by this violence against the present. ...Violence in everyday behaviour, violence against the past that is emptied of all substance, violence against the future, for the colonial regime presents itself as necessarily eternal.[49]

The violence of colonialism is not a problem of the past, as Fanon makes clear here; colonialism is embedded within the fabric of any society upon which it stamps.

Although Tambu cannot always articulate injustice beyond its direct relationship to her own experience, she is aware of the suffocating entrenchment of racism and sexism that are exacerbated by colonialism. Tambu's frustration at her inability to 'progress' comes to a head in the third novel, fuelling her anger which turns outwards to focus upon the younger generation and their perceived advantages. Unhappily employed as a high school teacher, Tambu bitterly notices that her 'pupils are all born frees' (born at, or near, the end of the war for independence), who 'expect more of the world than you ever dreamed the planet contained'. Their confidence 'ignites a smouldering resentment, a kind of grudge' within her.[50] One may expect the target of Tambu's eventual outburst to be Esmerelda, since she is a student who embodies the confidence and assuredness Tambu begrudges the younger generation. In fact, Tambu's internalized violence is unleashed upon the head of Elizabeth, 'a meek girl' whose parents are struggling to keep up with rent, never mind school fees.[51] In other words, Tambu may be lashing out externally but the target of her violence appears to be herself: Elizabeth is symbolic of Tambu's younger, determined self, before she was crushed by the racism and misogyny that obstructed any chance of success.

Tambu's violent act is horrific but there is an inevitability about her lashing out. From an early age, she has been discriminated against due to her gender and her blackness. What is the 'rational' response to realizing that society is rigged against your very existence? At the end of *Nervous Conditions*, Tambu-as-narrator recounts: 'I was young then and able to banish things, but seeds do grow. ... Quietly, unobtrusively and extremely fitfully, something in my mind began to assert itself.'[52] By *This Mournable Body*, Tambu *knows* what is feeding her various nervous conditions, making the *njuzu* bloat ever larger and provoking the hyena within to cackle. *This Mournable Body* reminds us that depression need not be 'silent, weary, numb' but may also be 'loud, agitated and intensely felt'.[53] Depression can be manifested and expressed in ways disruptive to societal norms, rather than simply being restricted to an individual, personal disruption.

A conclusion: the road to recovery

Dangarembga's Tambu trilogy offers no concrete, actionable 'solution' regarding how to decolonize the depressed mind. But there are gestures towards what it might take for alienated subjects to survive in the colonial world. *Nervous Conditions* and *This Mournable Body* both feature a public ceremony involving Tambu's mother, both of which result in Tambu confronting her ethical boundaries. In the first novel, it is the forced wedding ceremony of her parents that causes Tambu to rebel by refusing to get out of bed. In *This Mournable Body*, it is another faux-'traditional' ceremony back in her home village, a ceremony that requires the participating women to be semi-naked. Tambu is part of an 'eco-tourism' company and has been asked to organize this sham ceremony to entertain clients. Her mother, understandably, becomes overwhelmed by embarrassment and disrupts the performance. The chaos and fallout leads Tambu to resign from the company. But what is surprising in this instance is that Tambu confronts the shame she feels and wishes to be reconnected with her family and wider homestead community. In a few whiplash paragraphs, Tambu is *becoming* reconciled and integrated within the community she has tried desperately to get away from. Her dissociative self appears to become less fragmented when she decides to become a more active part of her community:

> [Christine] says, your education is not only in your head anymore: like hers, now your knowledge is now also in your body, every bit of it, including your heart ... This is the small first step toward maintaining your knowledge in the location of which Christine spoke.[54]

At the conclusion of *This Mournable Body*, Tambu's mind and body appear to be on the way to union. This belated 'dis-alienation' of Tambu's sense of self is not necessarily 'freedom' but is a gesture to a recovery of selfhood. The trilogy embodies what might be identified as Fanon's 'essential aim', according to Jean Khalfa and Robert J.C. Young: 'namely, to think and construct freedom as *disalienation* within a necessarily historical and political process'.[55] With its second-person narration and the culminating events of the novel, *This Mournable Body* destabilizes the trilogy's focus on the individual, underlining Fanon's argument that 'colonialism has not simply depersonalized the individual it has colonized; this depersonalization is equally felt in the collective sphere'.[56] The importance placed on the return to 'the collective sphere' at the end of the trilogy adds to the subversive potential of depression in a colonial context. Whether or not Tambu continues her somatic education towards liberation of the mind and heart is a process that looks likely to remain 'off the page' for the reader. For us, what it means to decolonize mental illness is an ongoing and continuous process in our world. May the hyenas and black dogs release us from their grip, so we can see the historical and political systems which feed them.

ACKNOWLEDGEMENTS
This essay began life as a part of the postcolonial strand organized by Clare Barker for the Northern Network for Medical Humanities Research conference in 2018. Many thanks to Clare for her continued support, to Frances Hemsley for observing the parallels between the *njuzu* in Dangarembga and Marechera, and Roxie Ablett for her insights on witch folklore.

NOTES

1. An example of the critical attention devoted to Nyasha, particularly to reading her disordered eating, is evident in her being the centre of many of the essays in *Negotiating the Postcolonial: Emerging Perspectives on Tsitsi Dangarembga*, eds, Ann Elizabeth Willey and Jeanette Treiber (Trenton, New Jersey: Africa World Press, 2002).
2. Clare Barker, *Postcolonial Fiction and Disability: Exceptional Children, Metaphor and Materiality* (Basingstoke: Palgrave Macmillan, 2012), p. 66.
3. Tsitsi Dangarembga, *Nervous Conditions* ([1988]; Banbury: Ayebia Clarke, 2004); Tsitsi Dangarembga, *The Book of Not* (Banbury: Ayebia Clarke, 2006); Tsitsi Dangarembga, *This Mournable Body* (Minneapolis: Graywolf Press, 2018).
4. Dangarembga, 'Interview with the Author', in *Nervous Conditions*, p. 209.
5. Jean-Paul Sartre, 'Preface' to Frantz Fanon, *The Wretched of the Earth*, trans. Constance Farrington ([1961]; London: Penguin, 2001), pp. 7-26.
6. Frantz Fanon, *The Wretched of the Earth*, p. 201.
7. Fanon, *The Wretched of the Earth*, p. 237.
8. Ann Cvetkovich, *Depression: A Public Feeling* (Durham and London: Duke UP, 2012), p. 12.
9. Cvetkovich, *Depression*, p. 12.
10. China Mills, *Decolonizing Global Mental Health: The Psychiatrization of the Majority World* (Hove and New York: Routledge, 2014), pp. 8, 9.
11. Dangarembga, *This Mournable Body*, p. 37.
12. Sartre, 'Preface' to *The Wretched of the Earth*, pp. 11, 12, 16, 17 (original emphasis).
13. As I've discussed elsewhere, Africa has a much longer history of cultural contact and movement within and outside of the continent prior to European interference: Amy

Rushton, 'No Place Like Home: The Anxiety of Return in Taiye Selasi's *Ghana Must Go* and Yvonne Adhiambo Owuor's *Dust*', *Études Anglaises*, 70:1 (2017) 45-62.

14. Even in the original French version of the preface, forms of 'you and 'your' ('vous', 'votre' and 'vos') appear approximately one hundred times: 'Préface à l'édition de 1961 par Jean-Paul Sartre', in Fanon, *Les damnés de la terre* ([1961]; Paris: La Découverte & Syros, Paris, 2002), pp. 17-36.
15. Dangarembga, *Nervous Conditions*, p. 1.
16. Dangarembga, *This Mournable Body*, p. 5.
17. Dangarembga, *The Book of Not*, pp. 3-4.
18. In *Nervous Conditions*, Maiguru – Nyasha's mother and Tambu's aunt – retreats to her bed soon after Tambu's arrival; Tambu's mother exhibits signs recognizable as postnatal depression; and Nyasha suffers a breakdown after Tambu leaves for the Catholic boarding school.
19. Dangarembga, *Nervous Conditions*, p. 152.
20. Dangarembga, *This Mournable Body*, pp. 36-7.
21. Cvetkovich, *Depression*, p. 20.
22. Fanon, *The Wretched of the Earth*, p. 40.
23. Dangarembga, *Nervous Conditions*, p. 168.
24. Dangarembga, *This Mournable Body*, p. 82.
25. Dangarembga, *This Mournable Body*, p. 82.
26. Dangarembga, *This Mournable Body*, p. 82.
27. Dangarembga, *This Mournable Body*, p. 83.
28. Dangarembga, *This Mournable Body*, p. 134.
29. Dangarembga, *This Mournable Body*, p. 134.
30. Dangarembga, *This Mournable Body*, p. 149.
31. Dangarembga, *This Mournable Body*, p. 5.
32. Grant Lilford, 'Traces of Tradition: The Probability of the Marecheran Manfish', in *Emerging Perspectives on Dambudzo Marechera*, eds, Anthony Chennells and Flora Veit-Wild (Trenton, New Jersey: Africa World Press, 1999), pp. 283-98, p. 286.
33. Dambudzo Marechera, *The House of Hunger* ([1978]; Illinois: Waveland Press, 2013), pp. 123-30.
34. Grant Lilford, 'Transformations of a Manfisch: Changing Allegories for the Njuzu in Shona Literature', *Journal des Africanistes*, 69:1 (1999) 199-219, p. 200.
35. Lilford, 'Traces of Tradition', p. 286; Lilford, 'Transformations of a Manfisch', p. 200.
36. Lilford, 'Transformations of a Manfisch', p. 200.
37. Dangarembga, *This Mournable Body*, p. 6.
38. Dangarembga, *This Mournable Body*, p. 101 (my emphasis).
39. David Lan, *Guns & Rain: Guerrillas & Spirit Mediums in Zimbabwe* ([1985]; Oxford: James Currey, 1999), pp. 35-6.
40. Lan, *Guns & Rain*, p. 36.
41. Dangarembga, *This Mournable Body*, p. 101.
42. Dangarembga, *This Mournable Body*, p. 149.
43. Dangarembga, *This Mournable Body*, p. 83 (my emphasis).
44. Dangarembga, *This Mournable Body*, pp. 94-8.
45. Lan, *Guns & Rain*, pp. 35-6.
46. Lilford, 'Traces of Tradition', p. 286.
47. Lan, *Guns & Rain*, p. 36.
48. Dangarembga, *This Mournable Body*, p. 199.
49. Frantz Fanon, *Alienation and Freedom*, eds, Jean Khalfa and Robert J.C. Young (London: Bloomsbury Academic, 2018), p. 654.

50. Dangarembga, *This Mournable Body*, p. 87.
51. Dangarembga, *This Mournable Body*, pp. 94, 97.
52. Dangarembga, *Nervous Conditions,* p. 208.
53. Amy Rushton, "'Who's Responsible –You Fucking Are'": Contesting Narratives of the Ongoing "Mental Health Crisis" in the UK', *Key Words*, 17 (2019) 87-108, p. 104.
54. Dangarembga, *This Mournable Body*, p. 284.
55. Jean Khalfa and Robert J.C.Young, 'General Introduction', in Fanon, *Alienation and Freedom*, p. 5.
56. Fanon, *The Wretched of the Earth*, p. 237.

Epidemic narratives of the Rwandan genocide: Health, memory, and testimony in Marie Béatrice Umutesi's *Surviving the Slaughter:The Ordeal of a Rwandan Refugee in Zaire*

FRANCES HEMSLEY

> The Rwandan tragedy is complex. There are not simply victims on one side (Tutsi) and guilty (Hutu) on the other as we have been led to believe. In our meetings we always proposed that all the guilty, regardless of their ethnicity, be identified, judged, and condemned for their crimes, and the innocent rehabilitated. Ignoring this reality would only impede progress towards reconciliation.[1]

The material and embodied health legacies of the Rwandan genocide (1994) are bound up with memory. During the April 7 commemorations, many taking part re-experience trauma through somatic manifestations, which in more chronic forms are expressed as, for example, *ihahamuka* (breathlessness).[2] Disease, disablement, and other epidemiological ramifications of the genocide act as forms of embodied memory. HIV infection preserves a direct link with the genocide, since systematic rape, a technique of ethnic cleansing, was deliberately weaponized to infect Tutsi victims. Increased incidences of malaria and tuberculosis have lasted far beyond the formal 'end' of the genocide. The genocide caused health problems that are marked on a collective corpus of people. Acknowledging this fact involves recognizing the way these health outcomes cut across lines of victim and perpetrator, most materially in terms of the communication of disease and the collective burden of disease across the population.

Equally, this acknowledgement means realizing that the composition of the population is not straightforward, as different sub-populations were exposed to different kinds of risks before, during, and after the genocide.[3] Those most affected include orphans, widows, and victims of rape and other forms of violence. Following the genocide, the exodus of Rwandan Hutus into refugee camps in the Democratic Republic of the Congo, where they lived without adequate shelter, food, water, sanitation, and humanitarian protection, gave rise to the worst cholera epidemics of the century. In addition, of the detainees awaiting trial in the first few years after the genocide, more died from infections and malnutrition than lived to be tried. These varied health impacts raise questions about how we disintricate and discriminate victims of epidemic from victims of genocide. To ask this question is to go beyond the now-customary observation that Hutu moderates were targeted during the genocide. It is instead to attempt to grapple with how we square the specific impact of genocide on a targeted ethnic group (the Tutsi) with more widespread health effects. This line of questioning is complicated even further when we take into account the impact of structural violence – the destruction of economies and infrastructure, including health infrastructure – during the genocide, and their startling recovery afterwards. Rwanda's post-genocide economic and social recoveries, including impressive gains in public health and an inclusive discourse of national reconciliation, have transformed its international standing.[4] Nonetheless, despite improvements in healthcare and numerous other public sectors since the genocide, Rwanda performs poorly according to international measures of human rights compliance and political freedoms. There is also the uncomfortable possibility that political hegemony, as well as social, economic, and health gains effectively absolve the Rwandan Patriotic Front (RPF) government of responsibility for possible war crimes during the Rwandan Civil War (1990-1994) and the First (1996-1997) and Second Congo Wars (1998-2003).[5] As Ananda Breed observes:

> Although Rwanda performs as a post-conflict society through a unified and non-ethnically-identified form of nationalism, it has committed ethnic violence in the Democratic Republic of Congo (DRC) against both Rwandan Hutu refugees and Congolese Hutu. Human rights abuses in the DRC do not discount or minimise the atrocities of the Rwandan genocide but the fact that there has been warfare based on ethnicity conducted by the government of Rwanda outside its borders while it performs ethnic unification within those borders poses questions concerning enactments of justice and reconciliation.[6]

Marie Béatrice Umutesi's testimonial memoir, *Surviving the Slaughter: The Ordeal of a Rwandan Refugee in Zaire*, attests to what happens 'after the end of' the genocide, and thus beyond the frame of the dominant post-genocide narrative of Rwanda's gains in health and discourse of national healing through reconciliation. Umutesi's text is carefully titled to emphasize her Rwandan nationality over her ethnic identity (Hutu). In *Surviving the Slaughter*, memory-work is heavily epidemiologically accented. Survivorship takes on new meaning in relation to the epidemiological burden experienced by Hutu refugees in Zaïre. In other words, 'survivor' is, for Umutesi, not exclusively applicable to the genocide and ethnicity (Tutsi as survivor): it is also to the wider circumstances of civilian endangerment. In the context of Hutu refugee camps, and the high epidemic risks associated with them, 'survivorship' becomes the ontological category around which memory and testimony is oriented. Reading Umutesi, I examine Rwandan genocide testimony in terms of these more dispersed and differentially distributed health impacts – or what I call, for the purposes of this article, alternative 'epidemic narratives' of the Rwandan genocide.

By using the phrase epidemic narratives, I wish to signal two things. The first concerns a trajectory of material health impacts; the second, a way the narratives of the Rwandan genocide are framed, that is, in a manner similar to epidemiological narratives which revolve around patterns of emergence, their spread and communication through carriers, and, finally, containment and cure. In 'What is an Epidemic?', Charles Rosenburg suggests that 'epidemics start at a moment in time, proceed on a stage limited in space and duration, follow a plot line of increasing and revelatory tension, move to a crisis of individual and collective character, then drift toward closure'.[7] The dominant narrative of the Rwandan genocide is similarly framed: the point of emergence for inter-ethnic hatred is generally located in the eugenic doctrines of the colonial administration – the so-called Hamitic hypothesis – or at the moment of transition from colonial administration to majority Hutu rule in 1962.[8] The narrative 'ends' with the RPF military victory and the containment of the genocide. If narratives of genocide, and epidemic, are end-oriented, then this raises the issue of what happens 'after the end' of such events.[9]

If one falls ill as an after-effect of genocide, does this form part of the 'narrative' of the genocide or a separate narrative about national (and extranational) health? How does the genocide, or the narrative of the genocide, invite categories of discrimination between the well and the ill – and how are health sequelae thought in terms of responsibility and guilt? A contemporary news report, 'A Week in Goma', by Robert Block for *The Independent*, causally linked the genocide and the refugee crisis in moral terms. Block collapsed the events of the genocide into those of the subsequent cholera epidemics, noting that 'The genocide may have stopped, more or less, but the torments of the people of Rwanda – self-inflicted and otherwise – continue in the cholera-ravaged refugee camps across the border in Zaire'.[10] This approach to the refugee crisis counterpoises distinct categories of victim – the victim of epidemic, the victim of genocide – and equates vulnerability, or perhaps more accurately, susceptibility, in which social contagion by genocidal ideology and bacterial infection by cholera are placed side by side, with guilt. In this way perpetrators of genocide become the victims of epidemic: 'The people who killed are now reaping the bitter harvest they have sown'.[11] The 'bitter harvest' Block imagines the génocidaires reaping is particularly scathing, given that malnutrition was, along with cholera, a primary cause of mortality during the refugee crisis. What I wish to signal here is the extimate role – exterior, yet intimate – epidemic has in the narrative of the Rwandan genocide. In this article, I explore the premise that epidemic narratives symbolically and materially tie together the events of the genocide of the Tutsi in Rwanda and their aftermath in DRC. Post-genocide health can nuance dominant narratives by taking into account the cultural construction of traumatic memory and its intersections with material health and perceptions of disease, transmissibility, and susceptibility. By paying attention to epidemic as both material fact and narrative event, we are forced to think beyond the 'end' of the Rwandan genocide in May 1994, a month after the genocide began.

Umutesi's testimonial memoir gives us an example of what René Lemarchand calls 'the clash of ethnic memories', an 'essential component of the process by which the legacy of the genocide – the "memory of the offense" – is being perceived and fabricated by one community or the other'.[12] By reading Umutesi's account as ethnic memory, I treat it as heavily nuanced, by which I mean to suggest that it offers a piercing, but necessarily partial and selective 'truth', characterized by shades of meaning and expression that are, at times, dignifying, compassionate, and humane, and, at others, indifferent and revisionist.[13] As Lemarchand notes, there inevitably exist 'distortions inscribed in the cognitive maps of both victims and perpetrators, that is, memory, in response to the exigencies of the moment'.[14] In Umutesi's account, such exigencies include those associated with the differential exposure to disease, malnutrition, and debilitation. *Surviving the Slaughter* reads as a dossier, documentary in its precision and reach, of the history and material conditions of complicated demographic fluctuations and displacements in Rwanda prior to the genocide, and in DRC just afterwards. The text catalogues the extreme deprivations of the camps: the inadequate sanitation and shelter, the lack of potable water, the wildly insufficient provision of nutrition, the exposure to infectious disease. It also documents the dynamics and processes of both grassroots community organizations, and of Rwandan and international NGOs. Because of the overwhelming epidemiological burden placed on those 'surviving' the camps, memory takes on an epidemiological accenting –

illness, exhaustion, and disease continually filter into Umutesi's account as both the most mundane and the most horrifying expression of the crisis. As well as direct mortality, disease means that young children are left alone and undiscovered inside plastic sheetings after the death of a parent or carer; disease means that money, which might otherwise be exchanged for food or used to barter for personal safety during times of flight, must be found to pay doctors or nurses in the camps; disease means that many are unable to eat less digestible foods, compounding the effects of malnutrition; disease means that those beyond the point of exhaustion are unable to continue fleeing and are left at the roadside to die. Umutesi recalls that '[w]hen someone was too sick to keep on walking he sat down by the side of the road and waited for death'.[15] Zuzu, a child Umutesi had taken into her care, and to whom the memoir is dedicated, 'died of exhaustion and malnutrition at Bombega'.[16] Elsewhere, remembering an older woman who had begun to improve her circumstances in the Kivu camps by acquiring a small business development loan from the Collective of Rwandan NGOs, Umutesi flatly observes: 'the four hundred kilometres that separated INERA and Tingi-Tingi were fatal to her. When she arrived at Tingi-Tingi she was exhausted and sick. Bad food and dysentery did the rest'.[17]

Umutesi's testimony defies easy categorization, partly because it automatically redefines our expectations about what Rwandan testimonial literature is, and who writes it. *Surviving the Slaughter* positions itself as the narrative of a Hutu 'survivor', and is therefore not readable within the dominant scripting of post-genocide identity and memory. As Breed notes, despite the ideology of inclusive 'Rwandanicity', in post-genocide Rwanda, the use of experiential categories in genocide memory tend to function as a form of ethnic categorization. Terms synonymous with Tutsis include victim, survivor, old returnees; those synonymous with Hutus include prisoner, perpetrator, new returnees.[18] Umutesi documents situational risks associated with ethnicity and perceived ethnicity that are by no means stable, and that are further complicated by a regional division between the North and the South. Umutesi attests to the not uncommon experience of risk associated with ethnic indeterminability:

> Since I came from Byumba in the North, I didn't feel very safe in Gitarama, where southern extremists could take advantage of the chaos that would follow the outbreak of war to get rid of the northerners. In addition, it often happened that I was taken for a Tutsi. If war came to Gitarama, I was in danger of being targeted by Hutu extremists who wouldn't hesitate to make the Tutsi pay for the attack by their refugee brothers. I knew that if the rebels [RPF] took power they would use the first few

days to get rid of bothersome Hutu. Being Hutu and in charge of an NGO, I had no hope of escaping the massacres.[19]

Umutesi is readable as both Hutu and Tutsi, and is 'misplaced' in terms of Rwanda's regional divisions. As such, she is at risk from different Hutu factions, and from the RPF, whom she terms 'the rebels'. In addition, Umutesi was no 'ordinary' civilian, but the manager of an NGO, and is therefore part of Rwandan civil society prior to the genocide. As such, her positionality is complicated by the imputation that civil society under President Habyarimana's single party state was by no means necessarily morally or politically neutral. As Johan Pottier observed in 1996, '[r]egarding Rwanda's NGOs in exile, the question is not only "who launched them?" and whether they were connected to the Habyarimana government, but whether they aligned themselves with "Hutu Power" extremists during the 1990-94 war and genocide'.[20] In the camps in Kivu, DRC, Umutesi undertook the reorganization of the Collective of Rwandan NGOs. The narrative framing of Umutesi's memoir reveals the influence of her NGO status; her concern with innocence over guilt is consistent with the way the Collective sought to represent the refugee crisis to the international community. Umutesi notes:

> We did not want to deny the presence of those who were guilty of genocide among the refugees ...We thought that the best way to marginalise the guilty was to recognise the existence of the innocent majority, thereby lessening the appeal of the génocidaires.[21]

This strategy occasions a tension – between recognition and denial – that is registered in the critical reception of both the Collective's manifesto and Umutesi's memoir. Pottier notes that:

> In its charter, the *Collectif des ONG* states that members are independent from the warring armies, the interim government (then in power), the RPF and political parties generally. While such neutrality may seem honourable, it is here noted that the *Collectif* advocates support to the displaced, but remains silent on the subject of genocide.[22]

The point here is that political neutrality risks looking like sectarianism when a recent genocide is not mentioned or denounced. Aliko Songolo similarly cautions that in her memoir 'Umutesi says relatively little about the role and influence of either Interahamwe or former Rwandan Army Forces (FAR) among the refugees in the several camps in which she lived', noting, nonetheless, that 'it is evident ... she was keenly aware of their presence'.[23] When Umutesi does mention the influence of the ex-FAR, it is to recall opinion circulating among the refugee community in ADI-

KIVU camp that militarization is the only solution to exile.[24] Increasingly, ex-FAR start to be treated as sources of protection.[25] This schism, in that one person's perpetrator of crime is another person's redeemer, takes on an added dimension in the knowledge that the provision of aid assistance is negatively affected by uncertainties about the extent to which ex-FAR and *Interahamwe* are represented among the refugee population and to what extent these forces control the camps. The problem for international aid donors, and for the Rwandan government, was the possibility that assistance might be redirected to those who had committed acts of genocide and who were planning an armed return to Rwanda. In response some agencies withdrew all their personnel and assistance in November 1994.[26]

Umutesi's narrative tends to position all Rwandan Hutu civilians, both within and outside of Rwanda, in terms of an ontology of vulnerability. A pervasive and shared ontological condition of vulnerability is inherent in bodily life, which, as Judith Butler observes, is 'both finite and precarious'.[27] In Umutesi's account this generalized condition of precariousness – the vulnerability and interdependence of bodies, their susceptibility to illness or injury, regardless of agency or powerlessness – is in tension with a more specific kind of precarity that is associated with but not exclusive to the experiences of the Hutu refugee community. In Butler's terms, precarity is that which is unevenly distributed: a condition experienced by the marginalized, the exploited, the endangered – those differentially exposed to insecurity, illness, violence, and death as a result of, for example, conflict or forced migration, even quarantine.[28] The exigencies of flight – shifting, situational, precarious – as Umutesi encounters death, disease, and disablement in the camps, on roads, and forest paths effectively evacuate the relevance of potential or actual guilt in the moment of encounter. Instead, the emphasis is placed on interdependence and survival, as well as on the needfulness and failures of international intervention. Complicated categories of discrimination – between the guilty and the innocent, the well and the ill, the perpetrator and the survivor – are simplified, in a sense, by an overriding distinction between those with and without proper agency. Those without agency are 'victims' on either side of the ethnic divide – and in Zaïre, it is Hutu civilians who are susceptible to the health impacts of the refugee crisis and vulnerable to injury by militant groups (nebulously termed 'rebels', highlighting, perhaps, a connection with the RPF in connection with whom Umutesi uses the term elsewhere). Umutesi's account offers an alternative epidemic narrative of the Rwandan genocide, which focuses on the specific conditions of precarity for Hutu refugees and locates responsibility for the failure to preserve life with the international community and with the United Nations High Commissioner for Refugees (UNHCR) in particular.

The conditions of precarity for Hutu refugees and the health consequences of the refugee crisis, are fundamental aspects of the way in which Umutesi makes the case for the 'innocence' of the majority of displaced Hutu civilians and their rights as political refugees. In Umutesi's account, the massacres of Hutu civilians within Rwanda by the RPF during the civil war that began in 1990, and of Hutu refugees in Zaïre by the Rwandan military-backed Alliance of Democratic Forces for the Liberation of Congo-Zaire (AFDL) from 1996 onwards, are compared to the acts of genocide against the Tutsi in Rwanda in 1994. In this light, we see how precariousness is 'not simply an existential condition of individuals, but rather a social condition from which certain clear political demands and principles emerge'.[29] Writing about the chaos of May 1994, which she spent working with other NGOs in Gitarama, Umutesi connects both Tutsi genocide and Hutu massacres with the culpability of the international community:

> In addition to the Tutsi genocide, which was happening before our eyes, the rebels undertook widespread killing of the civilian Hutu population in the zones that they occupied. Thousands of the people, the majority of them women and children, roamed the streets without any humanitarian aid. All of the humanitarian organizations had abandoned the country at the point when the Rwandan people needed them most. …The international community seemed more interested in gross acts of war than in the plight of the people who were being killed every day, of those who were hiding in the ceilings, woods, ditches, swamps, and of those thousands who were wandering along the roads. The weak, children, pregnant and nursing mothers, and old people who were condemned to die of starvation, sickness, and exhaustion.[30]

Here, something frictional happens in terms of the attribution of guilt and innocence. Umutesi attributes guilt to the 'rebels' (RPF) for massacres of Hutu civilians. The RPF are, even at the height of the Tutsi genocide, depicted as 'occupying' certain zones. So, while the RPF are treated as agents who undertake killings, the Tutsi genocide is referred to in the passive voice – it 'was happening' – in a manner that does not implicate those responsible. As the passage continues, Tutsi civilians targeted by the genocide and Hutu civilians are rendered one 'people', who are mutually defined by their 'plight'. This connection is fomented by the seamless transition between those in 'hiding', generally the only means of survival for Tutsis during the genocide, and those 'wandering', more applicable to the displaced Hutu civilians. By the final sentence of the passage, any distinction between Hutu and Tutsi suffering is overridden by the generalized experience of extreme vulnerability.

In accounting for the health crises faced by the Hutu refugees, Umutesi suggests a tipping point in the necropolitics of the Rwandan situation. The progress of the RPF towards the capital produces a preliminary refugee crisis as internally displaced Hutu civilians from towns along the Ugandan border through to Byumba prefecture start to gather outside Kigali. Umutesi recalls that in February 1993, the road from Byumba to Kigali is an 'uninterrupted river of refugees', a 'flood of displaced people'.[31] In these moments, she moves between testimony and secondary witnessing:

> Beginning in 1991, the RPF changed its military strategy. It abandoned conventional warfare for guerilla warfare. For the population of Byumba, the guerilla war could be bloody. Although at the start the rebels did not attack the civilian population, after 1991 they began to systematically kill them. People began to move en masse to the areas as yet unaffected by fighting. They told of atrocities committed by the rebels. Women were disemboweled, men impaled. ...These macabre stories created terror in the towns on the frontiers with Uganda. The rebels were no longer considered human. They were shown with horns and a tail, just like the devil in catechism books. I began to hear talk of the atrocities committed by the RPF when the first displaced people from the border towns arrived at my house in 1992. I had at first thought that these were fictions, products of the minds of people traumatized by two years of wandering.[32]

Here, alongside this act of secondary witnessing, Umutesi also attests to the way in which acts of violence become stories of violence, and the way in which both function to 'move' people, both physically and emotionally – across borders, and into separate 'camps'. With their transformation into stories these acts of violence become communicable, a form of social contagion entrenching fear and inter-ethnic hatred and tensions. The particular symbolism of these crimes against humanity has a complicated history: it circulates discursively, part of the imaginary of anti-Tutsi propaganda and features in different ethnic conflicts in the wider region. During both the 1972 pogroms against Hutus in Burundi, and again during the genocide of the Tutsi in Rwanda, many victims were impaled. In Rwanda before the genocide, impalement as a means of torture and putting-to-death formed part of the imaginary of extremist anti-Tutsi propaganda which circulated in the popular literature of Hutu extremism. This kind of literature was exploding in Rwanda between 1990 and 1994, and Christopher Taylor notes that the emergence of eighty new popular journals in this period is 'quite extraordinary for a country with a population of about seven million'.[33] Umutesi's account of the transformation of the RPF into 'signs' – 'shown with horns and a tail' – crucially does not identify the source of these representations, nor their means of circulation, but her emphasis on visual representation is suggestive of the images appearing in the many inexpensive political magazines published in Rwanda prior to the genocide. I do not mean here to suggest that atrocities of this nature did not happen, but to note that at moments like this, there is in Umutesi's account an instability in the 'source' of testimony, as we slip from testimony and secondary witnessing towards popular representations of Tutsis that have a place in genocidal ideology and that may be in part fabular – something the phrase 'macabre stories' also hints at.

In recording the 'systematic' massacres that led to the refugee crisis and in documenting the dire situation in the displaced-persons camps, both within Rwanda and in DRC, Umutesi alludes to continuities between deliberate campaigns of ethnic cleansing and the health consequences of the refugee crisis. Umutesi draws on a representational language that signals the proximity between her testimony and genocide testimony. This is particularly evident in the titling of Chapters 3 and 5, 'Surviving the Camps in Kivu' and 'The Death Camp at Tingi-Tingi', which shows a connection between genocidal processes and epidemic processes in the refugee camps. The public health crisis in the camps in Rwanda indexes a 'nonchalance towards death that does not necessarily seek out killing as its primary aim' but that instead starts to operate through disablement associated with malnutrition and infectious disease.[34] Umutesi recalls:

> With the offensive of February 1993, the RPF controlled almost all of Byumba prefecture ... more than 500,000 people had found shelter in refugee camps, where they lived in inhuman conditions. In these makeshift camps, where tens of thousands of the dispossessed were crowded, the hygiene was abominable. The latrines were not emptied. ... Every day epidemics of cholera and dysentery carried off several dozen people, especially children and the more vulnerable women. Most of the children were skeletal. Young girls looked like women a hundred years old. They were so thin their bones stuck out. ... Children, nursing and pregnant women, and old people died like flies of malnutrition.[35]

The displaced are at the lowest end of another scale of hierarchicalized bodies of interest within Rwanda (another scale works to place Tutsi at the lowest end as 'cockroaches' in need of eradication). Umutesi reveals how the refugees' condition of 'death-in-life' is treated as collateral, but also how susceptibility and vulnerability are coded as culpability, because of the regional and ethnic divides within Rwanda. Umutesi remembers one women's lack of empathy: 'For her it was fitting that these women and children suffer in their turn the anguish of exile'.[36]

In the passage above, the skeletal and prematurely aged appearance of starved and malnourished bodies inevitably evokes the conditions in the Nazi death camps during the Holocaust. In a later passage, Umutesi offers a more decisive, but still not explicit, connection between the refugee situation and the genocide, describing a Hutu woman whose Tutsi husband was killed in the genocide as a 'walking skeleton'.[37] This moment signals not only the intimate connections between Hutu and Tutsi, but also the way long-term processes of ethnic cleansing are generally marked on the bodies of the target-groups, who may be under-nourished and without access to health care. The expression 'died like flies' is frequently used in connection with the camps, and the association between heightened susceptibility to disease and flies signals the way in which refugees are made into a kind of vermin being, likened to the very insects that are a source of contagion. Indeed, Umutesi underscores the association between flies and epidemic risk: 'Since there were swarms of flies everywhere, I was concerned about fly-borne diseases'.[38] The idea of epidemic risk associated with unhealthful and fly-ridden environs characterizes her depiction of Tingi-Tingi:

> The camp was built on an unstable swamp. ... The climate was perfect for the proliferation of mosquitos and every kind of microbe. The water was a dirty yellowish colour. ... People arrived exhausted and famished, with swollen feet, hoping to find food and care. They were welcomed by a blazing sun and disease. The health of the refugees was already compromised by the long march and malnutrition. In this filthy swamp, epidemics of malaria, dysentery, and cholera ravaged them. They died like flies. ... It was times like this that I hated the international community, which had abandoned us at the moment we most needed them. ... I had heard that some countries and international organisations had even declared that there were no more Rwandan refugees in the eastern part of Zaire, apart from some Interahamwe and their families who deserved, it seems, their fate. Nonetheless there were more than a hundred thousand people at Tingi-Tingi.[39]

Here, Umutesi addresses head-on the logic of epidemic as retribution that characterizes the *Independent* article, 'A Week in Goma'. The logic of epidemic as a means of social purging is identical with that of ethnic cleansing. Here, Umutesi's transition from the politically specific 'Interahamwe and their families' to a humanized body count of 'a hundred thousand people' works to highlight the epidemic proportions of the crisis, and the disposability of the refugee community as a whole. Finally, while the phrase 'died like flies' tells of the objective conditions of heightened mortality, it also points to the dehumanizing anonymity-in-death that has become a condition of life in the camps. Umutesi recalls:

> When someone died, we wrapped him in a white *pagne* donated by Doctors Without Borders and took him to the cemetery, carried on the shoulders of four men. Every time I came across a cortège ... I would glance at the body to see if it were a child or an adult they were taking. Often the *pagne* didn't cover the feet of the dead person and you could see the toes and the soles of the feet.[40]

What is startling here is how similar this action is to the protocols of epidemiology researchers in the camps, who paid body collection agencies and healthcare centres to take anonymous death counts – differentiating only between children and adults.[41] Umutesi's impulse to record is connected to the trauma of her inability to take effective action: 'I watched their children die like flies without being able to do a thing'.[42] Later, in the camps in DRC, traumatic memory takes on an epidemiological accenting: 'I had nightmares. I saw refugees falling like flies from an unknown sickness. I awoke with a start thinking about what would become of us if humanitarian aid didn't arrive within a few weeks'.[43] In this moment, the desire for intervention is unconsciously connected with the epidemiological outbreak narrative: the 'unknown sickness' suggests the need for diagnosis and treatment, and the potentially catastrophic outcomes of the international community's failure to contain this new and deadly source of contagion.

Surviving the Slaughter attests to the way in which the sequelae of the genocide over-spill national borders, and international attempts at containing humanitarian crisis. In this way, Umutesi re-presents the legacy of the genocide by focusing on the crises faced by Hutu communities: crises of internal displacement, ethnic cleansing, and exodus. In ways that are not always entirely comfortable, Umutesi's account effectively decentres the 'unimaginable' event of the Tutsi genocide to concentrate on the origins of the Hutu refugee crisis, which she locates in 1991, during the first stages of the civil war within Rwanda initiated by the Rwandan Patriotic Front. In *Surviving the Slaughter*, the overriding question that Umutesi poses is simple: 'What crime had all of these victims committed to deserve such a death?'.[44] Umutesi suggests ultimately that reconciliation will not be possible unless 'all the guilty, regardless of their ethnicity, be identified, judged, and condemned for their crimes, and the innocent rehabilitated'.[45] Umutesi's mobilization of epidemic narratives to relativize the categories of innocence and guilt continue to be of relevance to the processes of reconciliation and memorialization in Rwanda and the wider region. In Rwanda, the Aegis Trust, an NGO that runs the major genocide memorials, advocates for the treatment of genocide as a preventable population health issue.[46] Aegis utilizes an epidemic narrative of genocide by comparing genocidal ideology to 'a spreading disease ... the end result of a preventable process'.[47] Indeed, there is a congruence between the Aegis Trust's representation of genocide and Umutesi's: Aegis redefines agency, while Umutesi relativizes it. There is undoubtedly a friction between the medicalization of genocide, on the one hand, and the material public health issues that affect victims, whether displaced peoples or survivors of genocide, on the other. However, by medicalizing genocide, or by remaining attentive to the wider health ramification of ethnic cleansing and its after-effects, it becomes possible to sidestep the question of guilt and innocence – a move which has the potential to be both highly problematic in terms of justice and helpful in terms of intervention and reconciliation. Ultimately, it might avoid the kind of abandonment that Umutesi describes when she testifies that the 'international community [which] had applauded the destruction of the camps in Eastern Zaire, ... abandoned us once again and let us wander in the forest like wild beasts and ... allowed this young girl of sixteen to collapse on the road like a dog, food for the ants of the equatorial forest'.[48]

NOTES

1. Marie Béatrice Umutesi, *Surviving the Slaughter: The Ordeal of a Rwandan Refugee in Zaire*, trans., Julia Emerson (Wisconsin: U of Wisconsin P, 2004), p. 73. First published in France in 2000 as *Fuir ou Mourir au Zaïre*.

2. Athanse Hagengimana and Devon Hinton, 'Somatic Panic Attack Equivalents in a Community Sample of Rwandan Widows Who Survived the 1994 Genocide', *Psychiatry Research*, 117 (2002) 1-9, p. 1; Christopher C. Taylor, '*Ihahamuka*: An Indigenous Medical Condition among Rwandan Genocide Survivors', *Oxford Handbooks Online* (Oxford UP, 2015) <https://www.oxfordhandbooks.com/view/10.1093/oxfordhb/9780199935420.001 .0001/oxfordhb-9780199935420-e-51> accessed 20 July 2019.

3. Dominique Legros, Christophe Paquet and Pierre Nabeth, 'The Evolution of Mortality Among Rwandan Refugees in Zaire Between 1994 and 1997', in *Forced Migration and Mortality: Roundtable on the Demography of Forced Migration*, eds., Holly Reed and Charles Keely (Washington DC: National Academy Press, 2001) 52-68, p. 52.

4. Madelaine Hron, 'Icyireze in Rwanda Fifteen Years Post-Genocide', *Peace Review*, 21 (2009) 275-9.

5. The Rwandan civil war commenced with the invasion of Rwanda by the Rwandan Patriotic Front, an elite corps of Rwandan Tutsi refugees in Uganda who had fought to bring Yoweri Museveni to power in the Ugandan Civil War. The civil war was designed to allow for the return of hundreds of thousands of Tutsi refugees in Uganda and Burundi. These people had fled the country during the transition from colonial administration to Hutu majority rule in the early 1960s, when there were waves of pogroms against Tutsi. The civil war ultimately forced the Hutu government (National Revolutionary Movement for Development, MRND) into peace negotiations with the RPF and domestic opposition parties. The negotiations were concluded with the

signing of the Arusha Accords in 1993. However, in 1994, President Habyarimana was assassinated and a full-scale genocide of the Tutsi began in Rwanda. The genocide was made possible by the premeditated arming and training of the Rwandan armed forces (FAR), Gendarmerie, and *Interahamwe* youth militias. In the countryside, most of the genocidal killings were carried out by civilians. At the conclusion of the genocide, a disastrous French military intervention, Operation Turquoise, allowed member of the FAR and *Interahamwe* to escape across the border into Zaire, along with Hutu civilians. Following the genocide, the RPF launched a series of military attacks aimed at disbanding the camps and disposing potential threats posed by génocidaires across the border. During the First Congo War, the RPF also backed what was effectively a proxy army, the Alliance of Democratic Forces for the Liberation of Congo-Zaire (AFDL), in toppling the dictatorial regime of Mobutu Sese Seko. This enabled the RPF to facilitate its pursuit of Rwandan refugees across Zaire.

6. Ananda Breed, *Performing the Nation: Genocide, Justice, Reconciliation in Rwanda* (Calcutta: Seagull Books, 2014), p. 3.
7. Charles Rosenburg, 'What is an Epidemic?', *Daedalus*, 118:2 (1989) 1-17, p. 2.
8. For a discussion of the 'Hamitic hypothesis', see Nigel Eltringham, *Accounting for Horror: Post-Genocide Debates in Rwanda* (London: Pluto Press, 2004) pp. 1-34.
9. Dora Vargha, *Polio Across the Iron Curtain* (Cambridge: Cambridge UP, 2018), p. 181.
10. Robert Block, 'A Week in Goma', *The Independent*, 31 July 1994.
11. Block, 'A Week in Goma'.
12. René Lemarchand, *The Dynamics of Violence in Central Africa* (Philadelphia: U of Pennsylvania P, 2009), p. 101.
13. Umutesi, *Surviving the Slaughter*, pp. 46-7.
14. René Lemarchand, 'Genocide in the Great Lakes: Which Genocide? Whose Genocide?', *African Studies Review*, 14:1 (1998) 3-16, p. 13.
15. Umutesi, *Surviving the Slaughter*, p. 164.
16. Umutesi, *Surviving the Slaughter*, p. 213.
17. Umutesi, *Surviving the Slaughter*, p. 151.
18. Breed, *Performing the Nation*, p. 13.
19. Umutesi, *Surviving the Slaughter*, pp. 19-20.
20. Johan Pottier, 'Relief and Repatriation: Views by Rwandan Refugees; Lessons for Humanitarian Aid Workers', *African Affairs*, 95 (1996) 403-429, p. 405.
21. Umutesi, *Surviving the Slaughter*, p. 74.
22. Pottier, 'Relief and Repatriation', p. 407.
23. Aliko Songolo, 'Umutesi's Truth', *African Studies Review*, 48:3 (2004) 107-119, pp. 115-6. Interahamwe were Rwandan youth militias, trained to perpetrate acts of genocide.
24. Umutesi, *Surviving the Slaughter*, p. 93.
25. Umutesi, *Surviving the Slaughter*, pp. 175, 181, 186.
26. Legros, Paquet and Nabeth, 'The Evolution of Mortality', p. 52.
27. Judith Butler, *Frames of War: When is Life Grievable?* (London and New York: Verso, 2009), p. 30.
28. Butler, *Frames of War*, pp. 25-31.
29. Butler, *Frames of War*, p. xxv.
30. Butler, *Frames of War*, p. 62.
31. Umutesi, *Surviving the Slaughter*, pp. 26, 27.
32. Umutesi, *Surviving the Slaughter*, p. 23.
33. Taylor, '*Ihahamuka*', p. 13.
34. Jasbir Puar, *Terrorist Assemblages* (New York: Duke UP, 2018), pp. 136-7.

35. Umutesi, *Surviving the Slaughter*, pp. 27-8.
36. Umutesi, *Surviving the Slaughter*, p. 33.
37. Umutesi, *Surviving the Slaughter*, p. 151.
38. Umutesi, *Surviving the Slaughter*, p. 76.
39. Umutesi, *Surviving the Slaughter*, pp. 144-5.
40. Umutesi, *Surviving the Slaughter*, p. 151.
41. Goma Epidemiology Group, 'Public Health Impact of Rwandan Refugee Crisis: What Happened in Goma, Zaire, in July, 1994?', *The Lancet*, 345 (1995) 339-44, p. 340.
42. Umutesi, *Surviving the Slaughter*, p. 29.
43. Umutesi, *Surviving the Slaughter*, p. 145.
44. Umutesi, *Surviving the Slaughter*, p. 73.
45. Umutesi, *Surviving the Slaughter*, p. 73.
46. Reva Adler et al., 'To Prevent, React, and Rebuild: Health Research and the Prevention of Genocide', *Health Services Research*, 39:6 (2004) 2027-51. In this paper, co-authored by James Smith, one of the founders of the Aegis Trust, it is emphasized that 'genocide-specific mortality rates are high, increasing, and far in excess of mortality rates for other catastrophic epidemics' (p. 2028).
47. Aegis Trust, 'What We Do. Our Starting Point', <https://www.aegistrust.org/what-we-do/our-starting-point//> accessed 09 July 2019. The Aegis Trust website presents their conceptual framing of genocide prevention diagrammatically, in a somewhat sanitizing three-phrase model drawing on primary, secondary, and tertiary preventative principles.
48. Umutesi, *Surviving the Slaughter*, p. 166.

MADELEINE LEE

small bites

i   bite

have you a poem on teeth
all my verse has bite
I chafe at the bit
taking the bait
most of us over-bite
most of us over-eat
most of us under-chew

less gatherer more hunter
incisors just miss lower teeth
enough to pinch or to clamp

what of those with under-bite
whose lower jaw exceed upper
who jam adverbs into a three-car collision

perhaps to console
the chinese say
an underbite jawline
depicts the scoop of wealth

ii   jaw

the orthodontist sawed off a chunk
of my goddaughter's lower jaw
and wired it for a fortnight
leaving her with a diet of
ice cream and soup

soon after in the car
on the way to a trinity college
med school interview
she suddenly changed her mind
opting for 5 years in dentistry

iii   **my mother has no upper teeth**

no wonder she feared the dentist
as a child a visit to a quack
removed an offending back molar
along with the rest of her upper gum
leaving her toothless post-infection

as a child on the dentist's chair
mouth agape i struggled wordlessly
unconsoled as i saw her cowering
in cold sweat in the brown linoleum-lined
waiting room with 60s mod-chic armchairs

as she turned eighty
we could hear her denture
clicking through peking duck treat
deformed gum
onto prosthetic
onto ceramic
onto duck breast
onto crown
onto good gum

would she become
like my grandfather
post-stroke at eighty-eight
demanding trenchantly
peking duck and given
a blended variation
instead on his hospital bed

iv   bird teeth

i was a talkative little girl
butting into every grown-up conversation
my granny called me bird teeth

birds have no teeth
early cretaceous creatures of flight
found in west china called confuciusornis
(being a chinese find) showed none

built between a modern pigeon and a kingfisher
predating the talkative label by
one hundred and twenty million years

v   swallow

late in his illness
my father asked for bird's nest soup
double-boiled and chilled

when served he gulped
his favourite dessert in
one swift swallow

thus was our outpour of affection
like martins' regurgitation

'Everything is a Search for Light': Indigenous Ageing and the Future of Intergenerational Wellbeing in Patricia Grace's *Chappy*

EMILY KATE TIMMS

I begin this article with a description of a popular political cartoon. Imagine three children building sandcastles on a beach. Suddenly, they look up and their mouths gape in alarm at a huge tidal wave looming over their heads, poised to sweep them away. The children see that the mass of grey water is made up of dangling limbs, glinting spectacles, walking sticks, wheelchairs, knitting needles, and permed grey hair. This apocalyptic scene, known as 'the silver tsunami', is depicted by Canadian artist Graeme McKay in reaction to the finding in Canada's 2016 census that older people now outnumber children.[1] The cartoon reflects 'statistical panic'; the worry that rapidly ageing populations are an impending global catastrophe.[2] The silver tsunami trope positions older people as an unstoppable natural disaster threatening to engulf younger people and, by implication, the futurity of the nation state.[3] McKay's cartoon is one example of how the pervasive metaphor of the silver tsunami depicts ageing as an existential – and one might also say transoceanic – threat in mainstream media in the US, Canada, the UK, and other countries in the 'Global North'.

The widespread fear of a silver tsunami is used to justify research into 'age-proofing' societies across the globe, from economists formulating ways to reduce dependency on expensive state pensions to medical researchers hoping to eradicate 'age-related' disease and disability.[4] The United Nations *Vienna International Plan of Action on Ageing* (1983) summarizes anxieties surrounding global ageing, stating that the 'implications of the aging of societies are for the time being largely negative ... unless serious and far-reaching efforts are made to turn this liability into a potential benefit'.[5] The implications of the silver tsunami trope – that age is synonymous with decline and that ageing populations disadvantage younger generations – are cause for concern. Ageing studies scholars and critical gerontologists address such problematic assumptions underpinning cultural rhetoric and gerontological research.[6] Margaret Morganroth Gullette, for example, argues that cultural metaphors indicate how older people are 'aged by culture'.[7] In short, cultural constructions of ageing have material consequences for older people when they are deemed to be 'too old', and they become subject to exclusionary ageist beliefs and controlling health and social policy programmes.[8]

Many contentious ageing policies are supported by mainstream gerontological theories. The most influential theory is that of 'successful' ageing, which 'emphasis[es] activity and productivity as a norm that the elder populace should strive to attain'.[9] To age 'successfully' requires older people to take responsibility for remaining healthy, free from disability, independent, and economically self-sufficient. Critical gerontologists and ageing studies scholars alike have criticized 'successful' ageing strategies for upholding the ethically dubious ableist, productivist, and individualist logics of neoliberal thought,[10] but the notion of successful ageing has gained political purchase as a solution for the 'problem' of the silver tsunami. The influential United Nations *Madrid International Plan of Action on Ageing* (1992), for instance, foregrounds 'successful' ageing strategies in order to stress that older people needed to 'take the lead in their own betterment' and 'participate actively' in society for 'as long as they are able to do so productively'.[11] Such policies and metaphors index what Cynthia Port identifies as the ageist 'reproductive futurism' of the Western 'cultural imagination', a belief that children symbolize the promise of the future and older people simply obstruct progress.[12] Given these policy and gerontological contexts, the silver tsunami metaphor delineates and naturalizes stark generational hierarchies between those valued as suitably 'young', autonomous, productive, and 'able', and the 'old' who are pejoratively characterized by dependency, decline, and disability.

A further problem which characterizes global ageing discourse, and which should be of interest to postcolonial scholarship, as I hope this article will bear out, is that the theory and policies of 'successful' ageing systemically ignore indigenous perspectives. Indeed, the *Madrid Plan* only refers to the '*recognition*' of the situation of ageing indigenous persons', which reads as a suspiciously aspirational statement regarding a meaningful engagement with the heterogeneous experiences and cultural values associated with indigenous ageing.[13] The apocalyptic visions of a silver tsunami contrast with indigenous perspectives in which elders are often viewed very positively. Older indigenous people are important contributors to their societies, with roles that include upholding cultural protocol and safeguarding histories, instigating resistance to colonial cultural assimilation, and leading contemporary activism on issues such as the pollution of natural resources.[14] Consequently, the recent call of First Nations scholar and activist, Sandy Grande, for 'a counter discourse and politics of ageing' informed by indigenous ontologies is necessary and overdue.[15]

At present, postcolonial approaches to age and ageing form a nascent field. Much existing work focuses on adapting postcolonial theoretical vocabulary to describe older people as marginal subjects. In 2016, contributions to a special issue of the *Journal of Aging Studies* draw on canonical postcolonial theory by Homi Bhabha, Gayatri Spivak, and Edward Said to 'open up new perspectives on the old person as "the other"'.[16] Another critical impulse is to 'decolonize' ageing studies and critical gerontology with recourse to 'indigenous' epistemologies from the Global South. These interventions, however well-meaning, tend to reductively exoticize indigenous thought, as demonstrated by Sweta Rajan-Rankin's enthusiastic declaration that researchers should 'reclaim older ways of knowing that predate and can form alternate discourses to western ways of knowing', or Peter Whitehouse's provocation that 'an enlightened Eastern perspective focusing on process, where truth, goodness, and beauty are more blended, can help age studies'.[17] Appeals to find precolonial perspectives on age risk lauding ossified – even romanticized – notions of race and culture by demanding that indigenous cultures provide 'authentic' alternatives to contentious Western narratives that frame ageing as an intergenerational catastrophe.

Whitehouse's work with Daniel George on 'intergenerativity' exemplifies how critical gerontologists draw on static concepts of indigeneity to theorize new models of elderhood and intergenerational relationships. 'Intergenerativity' describes 'opportunities created by aging and other human activities to bring forth experiences, stories and potential wisdom gained by an individual ... to create something new' with other generations by transferring repositories of experience. The theory aims to foster 'healthier' futures and uses unspecified indigenous conceptions of collective health to make the case that intergenerational stories are 'powerful healing forces' within an 'intergenerative' framework.[18] Whitehouse and George's theory of 'intergenerativity' requisitions 'indigenous' perspectives to present an idealized notion of the intergenerational transmission of knowledge. Their blunt dismissal that research on the nuances of 'intergenerative' relations 'would likely be a waste of time' overlooks an ethical priority to safeguard everyone involved in intergenerational exchanges; a priority that is often embedded in indigenous health and wellbeing frameworks.[19] Whitehouse and George's over-simplistic argument that older peoples' 'anecdotes (undocumented stories) can become antidotes' to global challenges fails to grasp the centrality and complexity of intergenerational collaboration, interdependence, and reciprocity to ontologies of indigenous wellbeing.[20] I argue that the grounds on which intergenerational relations are formed and nurtured is of paramount importance and requires investigation, especially given the legacy of historical and ongoing colonialism on wellbeing in indigenous communities.

This article challenges the logic of the 'silver tsunami' trope and reductive understandings of 'intergenerativity' through an analysis of the novel, *Chappy*, by the renowned Māori author, Patricia Grace.[21] I foreground a postcolonial approach to reading age and intergenerational relationships that engages with Māori ontologies of kaumātuatanga [elderhood] and indigenous health research. These counternarratives are dramatized through Grace's exploration of the processes by which intergenerational contact and collaboration enable elders to safely relate traumatic colonial family histories. Grace counteracts the notion that older people have a negative impact on younger generations by examining the enduring effects of colonial dispossession within the Māori community, and shows how older people rearticulate the means by which indigenous health futures can be secured. Consequently, my reading complicates the naturalized age-based hierarchies apparent in gerontological discourse as well as reductive interpretations of 'intergenerativity' in ageing studies and critical gerontology.

Kaumātua [elders] are usually older members of Māori iwi [tribal or kinship groups] with particular social and cultural responsibilities, and have played significant activist roles against Pākehā [New Zealander of European descent] colonial rule and governance.[22] The principles of kaumātuatanga are far removed from the neoliberal tenets of the 'successful' ageing paradigm. Mason Durie outlines how elders are implicated in models of Māori health such as the Whare Tapa Whā [four-sided house] model, in which connection to whānau [extended family] sits alongside mental, physical, and spiritual health as a vital precursor for health and wellbeing.[23] Kaumātua safeguard communal health – specifically younger generations' mana [spiritual power] and their association with whānau – and partly meet these obligations by passing on intergenerational knowledges and performing significant ceremonial and oratorical duties. In return, kaumātua can depend on their whānau for care and protection.[24] Effective intergenerational relations between kaumātua and younger people, based on interdependence and reciprocity, are vital for collective health and wellbeing as well as the cultural survival and continuity of Māoritanga [the Māori way of life]. Collective wellbeing is contingent on complex caring dynamics between the elder and other generations in the whānau, and is not reducible to the transference of an older person's repository of stories.

Chappy is set in 1985 and comprises a multigenerational account of the Star whānau living in a rural Māori community near Wellington. The narrative begins by following Daniel, the son of a Danish financier and a Māori translator, who has received a privileged upbringing in Switzerland. After he attempts to commit suicide outside his German University, Daniel is sent to live with his maternal Māori grandmother, Oriwia Star. In Aotearoa New Zealand he becomes fascinated by his deceased grandfather, Chappy, a Japanese stowaway who was subsequently adopted by the Star kaumātua and married Oriwia. To find out more about his grandfather, Daniel interviews his grandmother and great-uncle Aki, Oriwia's brother by adoption and the whānau's contemporary kaumātua. As Aki and Oriwia reveal layers of ancestry, the narrative ranges between the archipelagos of Aotearoa, Hawai'i, and Japan, making the Star whānau's diasporic histories increasingly apparent. Grace establishes the connection between kaumātua, whakapapa [genealogy or genealogical knowledge], and intergenerational health as Daniel links his discoveries about Chappy's past with his own wellbeing: 'When I began thinking ... about finding out about my grandfather, I became interested by what I now saw ahead of me – an opportunity to piece bits of *myself* together'.[25] After experiencing the ameliorative effects of learning his whakapapa, Daniel collates Aki and Oriwia's narratives into an account to be read by the family.

Chadwick Allen argues that Grace's earlier fiction strategically deploys 'idealized' representations of kaumātua-grandchild relationships through the 'scene of intergenerational instruction'. These bonds are predicated on elders divulging knowledges so that younger Māori 'may lay claim to their cultural inheritance' and assert a collective indigenous identity specifically tied to the land [whenua] to 'secure the creation of a future as *Māori*'.[26] Allen's interpretation of the symbolic value of kaumātua, while grounded in a specific cultural context, is not so far removed from Whitehouse and George's theory of intergenerativity. Like Whitehouse and George, Allen suggests that the transference of stories is the key role of kaumātua in securing community wellbeing. Both inadvertently propagate different, but no less hierarchical, depictions of intergenerational relationships that value older people for passing on knowledge or stories.

I counter these claims to argue that in *Chappy*, Grace's representation of intergenerational relations spanning five generations of the Star whānau sets up a dynamic relationship between kaumātuatanga and collective indigenous wellbeing in Māoritanga. Elders, in this text, develop a nuanced understanding of health as a process of transoceanic connection that enables them to circumvent patterns of illness transmitted across generations. Such understandings facilitate fresh collaborative opportunities for old and young alike to pursue healthy futures.

In *Chappy*, Grace stakes out a sophisticated understanding of intergenerativity by emphasizing processes of mediation and the need for safety when divulging genealogical knowledge. Much valuable criticism on Grace's oeuvre focuses upon how storytelling is figured as a means to confront inherited colonial trauma.[27] Yet Grace is cautious not to romanticize indigenous storytelling practices as an unqualified panacea.[28] Narrating is by no means a painless task for kaumātua in *Chappy*: it is freighted with physical and emotional demands, especially when relating distressing or traumatic circumstances. Grace dwells on informal processes of mediation to mitigate the potential dangers of storytelling to an elder's health and wellbeing.

Aki remembers one instance of mediation where his grandfather Paa, as part of his duties as a kaumātua, was expected to perform whaikōrero [a formal speech]. Paa had returned with Aki's father from a fruitless search for Aki's missing infant brother, Marama. The physical exhaustion incurred from the gruelling trek, combined with the emotional distress at failing to recover the child, took a great toll on the old man, reducing him to a 'formless individual'.[29] When the time arrives for the elder to formally relate Marama's fate to the whānau, Aki's father assumes the speaking responsibilities. He stands behind Paa with one hand on his father's chair 'to show everyone that he was not being disrespectful in standing to speak ahead of his elder, but that it was his intention to take the burden from the older man'.[30] Traditional protocols of the father speaking before the son are nullified in instances where elders are unable to stand and talk.[31] Aki's father does not usurp or take his father's place, but is sensitive to the physical demands that oratory and storytelling can place on elders. This act of oral mediation, facilitated by intergenerational physical contact, constitutes a wellbeing safeguard and becomes part of 'the protocols [Aki] learned little by little during [his] life'.[32] Māori protocol is shown to be flexible, accommodating elders' physical wellbeing within a set of reciprocal relationships designed to facilitate their continuing participation in important whānau activities.

These practices of intergenerational mediation are woven into the fabric of the novel's narrative structure and form, which comprises Aki and Oriwia's genealogical stories, Daniel's written introduction and epilogue, and his recollections of conversations with his great-uncle and grandmother. *Chappy* differs from Grace's earlier novels such as *Baby No-Eyes*, which are often premised on a collective decision among family members to directly deliver their accounts to each other, so that the narrative structure is reminiscent of a hui [communal meeting]. There are also instances of recording elders' stories in *Baby No-Eyes* to preserve histories for future activism. But in *Chappy*, the narrative is entirely facilitated through Daniel's separate recorded interviews with Aki and Oriwia. The story of Chappy is not, therefore, told all at once, or even told directly by one family member to another. Aki reiterates his grandfather's situation by using his nephew's tape recorder as an informal means of mediation, which enables him to relay sensitive and distressing familial histories to the family, stories rooted in the racialized and exclusionary histories of colonization. He articulates as yet untold stories about his courtship of the Native Hawaiian woman, Ela, and her family's eviction from their kalo gardens by US cash-cropping agricultural industries, as well as her public humiliation when the American father of her son, Lani, urinated on her cooking fire.[33] These colonial historical and familial grievances are so significant that Aki feels 'stabbed' to hear 'about something so dreadful, so personal and shaming'.[34] Given the distressing nature of these genealogical stories, Oriwia speculates that 'maybe he finds it easier to say things to a machine'.[35] The tape recorder acts as a technological mediator, enabling Aki to relate traumatic and sensitive familial histories for the first time. Grace's novel shows how indigenous oratorical practices might be altered to accommodate threats to elders' emotional wellbeing presented by distressing episodes in family and colonial history.

The narrative structure could appear to resemble the confessional genre, with elders' private, one-on-one recording sessions being edited into a volume by the grandchild. However, Daniel also plays a mediating role as he goes between elders to record their perspectives before playing them to the whānau. Aki's insistence on speaking in te reo [the Māori language] requires Oriwia to translate his recordings for Daniel, meaning that his narratives also become mediated through translation and transcription by another older person. Cycles of private recording and public transcription move the narrative structure away from a confessional mode as the stories are always intended to be heard. In addition to her transcription duties,

Oriwia uses the mediated qualities of recording and playing stories separately to establish a dialogue with her brother. It is well-known in the narrative that Oriwia opposed Aki's marriage, and he has consequently avoided discussing Ela with the whānau after her death from breast cancer. Oriwia records a story of a jealous aunt who makes her niece ill through the power of muttering curse words, emphasizing that she did not feel any such ill-will to her sister-in-law, especially 'the deep, affecting kind which can knock people down in their tracks'.[36] She tells Daniel to play the story to Aki so that 'he knows that what happened to Ela was nothing to do with me' and tells her brother that 'it's what I've started to say ... but you always cut me off'.[37] If Aki finds himself more able to *speak* genealogical stories into a machine, Oriwia makes the case that it may sometimes also be easier for elders to *hear* stories played from the device as opposed to direct communication. She hopes that the story will exonerate her from being implicated in Ela's cancer diagnosis and will elicit her brother's forgiveness decades later. Grace's narrative structure refracts the motif of the scene of elder instruction or notions of 'intergenerativity' into subtle processes of mediated storying, animated by intergenerational cooperation and contact within a community sensitized to the risks to a kaumātua's wellbeing that stories can pose. Successful mediation of storytelling, in turn, generates opportunities for intra- and inter-generational reconciliation and for younger people and other older people to protect elders' wellbeing as they relate whakapapa and fulfil cultural duties.

The intergenerational mediation dramatized by the novel's structure and form subsequently enables older people to reshape understandings of illness, particularly in relation to the enduring effects of colonialism on indigenous wellbeing. These reflections take place when, after listening to Oriwia's story, Aki recalls his life with Ela in Hawai'i and her experience of living with terminal cancer. Grace's metaphors describing illness in *Chappy* engage the concept of inherited colonial trauma to complicate the common assumption, as asserted by Allen, that connections to land promote indigenous health.[38] Māori health researchers, Rebecca Wirihana and Cherryl Smith, explain that inherited colonial trauma is a material process whereby the systemic degradations of colonial rule manifest themselves in collective contemporary indigenous health conditions. Individual illness in the present can feasibly be attributed to collective disadvantages accumulated over generations.[39] Both clinical vocabularies of 'tumour' or 'treatment' and traditional beliefs that sickness can be caused by ill-will ultimately prove insufficient in accounting for

Ela's illness.[40] Instead, as he describes the causes of Ela's tumour, Aki draws on the intergenerational knowledges of his elders, who stress the impact of colonization on mental, physical, and whānau health, and liken illness to a germinating plant:

> What I did not put enough thought to at the time were the effects of underlying anxiety or hurt – the invisible distress that people live with every day. This is grief and loss, or the threat of it, which works its way through whole communities down through decades. It's a communal distress, which lodges somewhere in the communal mind. It hides unnourished until somewhere, in someone or some people, it dislodges to live in the physical body. Once there, it is fed. It has roots within it which begin to seek out their own life blood. It has tendrils which branch in every direction in search of light. Everything, everything is a search for light.
>
> In listening to myself speak of this, I hear the voices of my mother and elders. I tell it their way because there's truth in it.[41]

Aki's description of 'communal distress' passed down through generations explicates the material reality of inherited colonial trauma. In stressing the 'truth' of his elders' words, Aki posits that Ella's 'lumps and bumps'[42] are an embodied manifestation of generations of land dispossession, impoverishment, and separation from traditional gardens, combined with the subtle grievances of day-to-day existence as a direct result of US imperialism in Hawai'i.

As Grace describes illness as a carnivorous, blood-sucking plant, the passage invites comparison with Allen's argument that the connection between Māori kaumātua, their grandchildren, and the land is integral to indigenous futurity. Contra Allen, Aki's description of illness via the trope of a germinating plant, far from asserting indigenous belonging and strength, conveys how colonial distress and sickness can become 'rooted'. Some roots, therefore, may be complicit in the perverse destruction of indigenous life. In consciously echoing the voices of his elders Aki repeats their stories to the succeeding generation. Aki passes on the knowledges of his ancestors but does not necessarily create an 'intergenerative' solution to the deep-seated health inequalities cultivated over generations of colonial rule. Māori intergenerational relationships are not romanticized as inexorably healing, since kaumātua can also pass on a genealogy of illness.

Of course, remembering and passing on stories of hurt and illness via whakapapa is a means of honouring in the present the memory of ancestors' colonial struggles. Yet Grace acknowledges the potential damage and hurt that stories can generate. The question arises naturally in the text of how elders might conceptualize health within intergenerational stories and storytelling practices without perpetuating illness. Older people in *Chappy* work their way out of this conceptual and material impasse by remembering instances where elders *synthesize*, as opposed to relate or transmit, knowledges, specifically through forming whakapapa. Grace draws attention to commonalities in genealogical practices performed by Native Hawaiian kūpuna [elders] and Māori kaumātua. Both cultures make use of what Elizabeth DeLoughrey terms 'strategic reconstruction', a process in which elders incorporate new families into whakapapa.[43] This is exemplified in parallel stories relating Aki's wedding to Ela, and Lani's marriage to Oriwia's daughter, Binnie. The events take place three generations apart from each other, but Grace puts these scenes together to show the shared practice of genealogical linking between Māori and Native Hawaiians. Aki tells Daniel how, at his ceremony, the kūpuna 'A'makualenalena recites a shared genealogy comprising 'names to do with the sailing and the venturing', which is echoed by Paa's speech at Binnie's wedding:

> My Hawaiian family were at once alerted when they heard the names that connected them in time and place with my home family, we of Aotearoa being junior to those left behind in the 'the great, far-distant, etched-on-the-heart, longed-for homeland of Hawaiki'.[44]

The strategies used by the elder to merge two distinct Pacific genealogies is reminiscent of the argument of Tonga-Fijian writer and activist, Epeli Hau'ofa, that common histories of migration and economic and cultural exchange connect Pacific communities in a 'sea of islands'.[45] I draw on Hau'ofa's configuration to contend that kaumātua and kūpuna in *Chappy* create a transoceanic genealogy as they recite and reform whakapapa to inaugurate new connections and forms of cross-cultural reach between Native Hawaiians and Māori. The term 'transoceanic' foregrounds the specific watery histories of migration and seafaring in the novel, given Aki's experience as a merchant sailor and the new affective connection with the ancestral homeland of Hawaiki on which the elders predicate their genealogical linking. Paa deprioritizes the metaphysics of Māori genealogical attachment to the whenua to reflect his family's diasporic nature and produce a transoceanic whakapapa. The novel's elders restructure intergenerational knowledges to accommodate other Pacific cultures, belying reductive interpretations that elders simply pass on self-contained knowledges.

Native Hawaiian elders in the novel also share parallel genealogical histories of the impact of Hawai'i's past of cultural and material oppression on indigenous wellbeing. As Aki cares for Ela during her terminal illness, 'A'makualenalena draws on ancestral knowledges and combines them with his own experience: 'he had his own memory of events, but added to that were the memories he had of all those who had gone on ahead of him'.[46] The elder concludes that Native Hawaiians are 'from a seed that was put into the ground at the time of creation …You live, you survive so your child can have life'.[47] The botanical image of the seed recalls Aki's description of inherited illness, but in this case asserts Native Hawaiians' ability to endure. Grace foregoes any aesthetic invocation of roots and concentrates on the metaphorical appeal to photosynthesis: 'Often you live in darkness, crushed and creeping about in search of light'.[48] Seeking light is framed as a means of finding ways to survive. The metaphor intermixes the rootedness of Native Hawaiian creation mythologies as a sovereign people planted into the ground with the routed necessity of movement to endure the ongoing damage of American colonization. The process of photosynthesis, in which the tendrils of the young plant search for light, is rearticulated as a metaphorical means to describe a search for intergenerational wellness.

The kaumātua and kūpunas' articulation of a historicized transoceanic affiliation, coupled with the latter's stories of intergenerational survival, inspires elders in the narrative present to revise their understanding of the impact of inherited colonial trauma on indigenous wellbeing. Aki synthesizes his ancestral knowledges with the words and deeds of his Hawaiian elders to gradually supplant aesthetics of botanical rootedness with images of light and oceanic voyaging. After Ela abandons her lonely and painful treatment at the local hospital, Aki accompanies her to visit the kūpuna and healer, Lili, who relieves his wife's pain by immersing her in healing waters. He remarks:

> to be well in spirit lifts the physical and mental state to an extraordinary level. …All are affected by it. Dark thoughts disappear.
> During those days of caring for Ela, my thoughts would often return to the time of my childhood when I would hear the old people say that we earthlings are related to the stars. The stars are our flesh and blood. I came to understand that this must be true in the deepest sense. We come from the dust of stars.[49]

The ancestral knowledges of Hawaiian elders and Māori reframe the rooted materiality of inherited illness with an understanding of wellness which links water, blood, and light. Lili's healing ritual of ka wai ola [the living water][50] and 'A'makualenalena's story of indigenous survival open new possibilities for indigenous health. Aki interweaves his memories with Māori creation cosmologies whereby the human race is born due to the separation of Ranginui [Sky Father] and Papatūānuku [Earth Mother], a severance that introduced light into the universe and created the stars used by the ancestors to navigate the seas from their homeland of Hawaiki to Aotearoa.[51] This new understanding of indigenous wellbeing is appropriate even in circumstances where 'health' appears to be at its most precarious: after the ceremony, Lili announces that Ela is 'well now'. Aki concurs as he tells Daniel 'What I can say about those words of Lili's, "she's well now"', is that I found them to be true. To be well in spirit is the most important health.'[52] The new aesthetic significance attributed to aquatic belonging and transoceanic movement means that *Chappy* does more than, as Leonie John suggests, 'feature an Oceanic genealogy'.[53] Rather, elders' knowledges are shown in the novel to be in constant intergenerational evolution within and between indigenous histories and cultures both before and since colonization. The kaumātuas' merging of Hawaiian and Māori ancestral knowledges marks a pivotal shift from reiterating the rooted historicization of inherited colonial trauma to asserting new collective metaphors for intergenerational wellbeing based on a connective cosmic genealogy of light and transoceanic movement.

As Aki creates new narratives of health and indigenous survival, he completes an intergenerational cycle wherein young and older members of the whānau create conditions for the safe telling of the elders' knowledges. In turn, the elders in the text synthesize intergenerational genealogical stories to devise new means of negotiating the inherited ills of colonial trauma. In the epilogue, Oriwia uses her brother's transoceanic understanding of collective wellbeing to guide a new intergenerational collaborative practice, whereby older people and their younger whānau attempt to recover whakapapa. Despite being the eponymous figure of the novel, Chappy had died before Daniel began his interviews, and there are considerable gaps in the Star whānau's knowledge of the Japanese grandfather. Oriwia explores how the family might generate new genealogical stories to account for Chappy's earlier life, and she plans with Daniel to leave Aotearoa to visit Hawai'i and Switzerland, before travelling with her grandson in Japan, so that she might reconnect with her extended family and find out more about her husband. Oriwia closes the novel by incorporating Aki's routed understanding of health with her collaborative search for genealogical stories: '"All time becomes one ... Everything's a search for light"'.[54] Aki's metaphorical alignment of health and wellness with transoceanic voyaging and light is requisitioned into a new project of cooperation between generations to construct whakapapa.

As these stories are destined to become a textual object for 'a whole whānau who would be intrigued if answers could be found',[55] Oriwia establishes a fresh collaborative literary practice to sit alongside oral storytelling. Animated by a pattern of intergenerational transoceanic voyaging and return, the synthesis of new genealogical narratives into an ever-expanding transoceanic whakapapa will benefit collective wellbeing.

Oriwia's closing words, laden with the promise of transoceanic voyaging as she prepares to cross the Pacific with her grandson to search for new genealogies, contrasts with the more alarmist, but no less aqueous, image of the silver tsunami epitomized by McKay's cartoon. Indeed, dominant depictions of old age as a tidal wave of decline, dependency, and threat to younger people, and the rhetoric of reproductive futurism, have never gained purchase in Grace's writing. *Chappy* is less concerned with rehabilitating elders from perceptions of decline and intergenerational conflict than with meditating on the kind of caring, inclusive and culturally connective communities that Māori wish to foster. My reading of *Chappy* asserts how Māori fiction can challenge ossified notions of indigenous wellbeing and uncritical understandings of 'intergenerative' transfer as currently conceived in critical gerontology and ageing studies. The conceptual move towards 'intergenerativity' creates new normative expectations for older people based on romanticized notions of transferring knowledges. 'Health', under these terms, is associated with an enduring connection with the land and the passing on of 'precolonial' ways of knowing. Grace's novel exposes the flaws in such thinking by showing how older people are points in a constellation of reciprocal communal relationships with younger generations. Crucially, to safeguard collective wellbeing, and hence the cultural continuity of Māoritanga, requires ongoing intergenerational mediation of Māori ontology, protocol, and informal cultural practices to facilitate the safe telling of elders' stories. Grace's figurative movement from indigenous roots to transoceanic routes demonstrates how elders are more than repositories of lived experience: they utilize whakapapa to reconfigure the transmission of colonial trauma into a healing navigation of transoceanic knowledges, which places a new and particular emphasis on the co-production of genealogical narratives between generations and indigenous Pacific cultural traditions. As such, Grace powerfully affirms the enduring importance of a nuanced engagement with indigenous ontologies of ageing and wellbeing, suggesting how indigenous elders might address the unequal, even traumatic, health legacies of colonial rule in the past and envision healthier futures for young and old alike.

NOTES

1. Graeme McKay, 'Seniors Outnumber Children in Canada', *Twitter*, 4 May 2017, <https://twitter.com/mackaycartoons/status/860198051859881984> accessed 06 April 2018.
2. Kathleen Woodward, *Statistical Panic: Cultural Politics and Poetics of the Emotions* (London: Duke UP, 2009), p. 14.
3. Andrea Charise, '"Let the Reader Think of the Burden": Old Age and the Crisis of Capacity', *Occasion: Interdisciplinary Studies in the Humanities*, 4:1 (2012) 1-16, p. 3.
4. Lauren Henderson, Bala Maniam and Hadley Leavell, 'The Silver Tsunami: Evaluating the Impact of Population Aging in the U.S.', *Journal of Business and Behavioural Sciences*, 29:2 (2017) 153-69, p. 164; Ankita Sarkar et al., 'Alzheimer's Disease: The Silver Tsunami of the 21st Century', *Neural Regeneration Research*, 11:5 (2016) 693-7, pp. 693-4.
5. United Nations, *Vienna International Plan of Action on Ageing* (New York: United Nations, 1983), p. 17.
6. Critical gerontology interrogates the premises of mainstream gerontology and is informed by anti-ageist activism, Marxist political economy, and social constructivism. Stephen Katz, 'Critical Gerontology for a New Era', *Gerontologist*, 59:2 (2019) 396-7, p. 396. The term 'ageing studies' was coined by Margaret Morganroth Gullette, and work in this field critiques the processes by which 'bodies are aged by culture more or at least equal to the biological fact of aging'. Margarette Morganroth Gullette, *Aged by Culture* (Chicago: U of Chicago P, 2004), pp. 6-7. Feminist scholarship was crucial to the development of ageing studies and scholars work with modes of cultural representation including photography, fiction, and television and also engage with philosophical and theoretical perspectives on, for example, care, retirement homes.
7. Gullette, *Aged by Culture*, p. 12.
8. Gullette, *Aged by Culture*, pp. 35-6.
9. Morten Hillgaard Bülow and Thomas Söderqvist, 'Successful Ageing: A Historical Overview and Critical Analysis of a Successful Concept', *Journal of Ageing Studies*, 31 (2014) 139-49, p. 142.
10. Lucy Burke, 'Imagining a Future without Dementia: Fictions of Regeneration and the Crises of Work and Sustainability', *Palgrave Communications*, 3:1 (2017) 1-9, p. 4; Toni Calasanti, 'Combating Ageism: How Successful is Successful Aging?', *Gerontologist*, 56:6 (2016) 1093-101.
11. United Nations, *Political Declaration and Madrid International Plan of Action on Ageing* (United Nations: New York, 2002), p. 11, p. 210. Henceforth *Madrid Plan*.
12. Cynthia Port, 'No Future? Aging, Temporality, History, and Reverse Chronologies', *Occasion*, 4 (2012) 1-19, pp. 3-4. Scholars tend to use 'Western' as a catch-all phrase to denote the 'Global North' and the Eurocentric origins of mainstream gerontology. The term strategically, and erroneously, constructs the 'West' as a homogenous entity.
13. UN, *Madrid Plan*, p. 18. My emphasis.
14. For example, see Anne Salmond, *Eruera: The Teachings of a Māori Elder* (Wellington: Oxford UP, 1980), p. 205; and Shirley Ida Williams Pheasant, '"That's My Bridge": Water Protector, Knowledge Holder, Language Professor', in *Unsettling Activisms: Critical Interventions on Aging, Gender, and Social Change*, eds, May Chazan and Melissa Baldwin (Toronto: Women's Press, 2018), pp. 80-88, p. 86.
15. Sandy Grande, 'Aging, Precarity, and the Struggle for Indigenous Elsewheres', *International Journal of Qualitative Studies in Education*, 31:1 (2018) 168-76, p. 169.
16. Silke van Dyk and Thomas Küpper, 'Postcolonial Perspectives in Aging Studies: Introduction', *Journal of Aging Studies*, 39 (2016) 81-2, p. 81.

17. Sweta Rajan-Rankin, 'Race, Embodiment and Later Life: Reanimating Aging Bodies of Color', *Journal of Aging Studies*, 45 (2018) 32-8, p. 36; Peter Whitehouse, 'Intergenerative Transdisciplinarity in a Future of Aging Professions: New Words Are Not Enough', *Age, Culture, Humanities*, 1 (2014) <http://ageculturehumanities.org/WP/intergenerative-transdisciplinarity-in-a-future-of-aging-professions-new-words-are-not-enough/> accessed 30 March 2017.
18. Peter Whitehouse and Daniel George, 'From Intergenerational to Intergenerative: Towards the Futures of Intergenerational Learning and Health', *Journal of Intergenerational Relationships*, 16:1-2 (2018) 196-204, p. 199.
19. Whitehouse and George, 'From Intergenerational to Intergenerative', p. 198. For an example of safeguarding in indigenous health frameworks see Ioana Radu, Lawrence M. House and Eddie Pashagumskum, 'Land, Life, and Knowledge in Chisasibi: Intergenerational Healing in the Bush', *Decolonization: Indigeneity, Education and Society*, 3.3 (2014) 86-105, p. 92.
20. Whitehouse and George, 'From Intergenerational to Intergenerative', p. 200.
21. Patricia Grace, *Chappy* (Auckland: Penguin Random House, 2015).
22. Ministry of Māori Development, *Oranga Kaumātua: The Health and Wellbeing of Older Māori People* (Wellington: Ministry of Māori Development, 1997), p. 10.
23. Mason Durie, *Whaiora: Māori Health Development* (Oxford: Oxford UP, 1998), pp. 69-73.
24. Mason Durie, 'Kaumātautanga Reciprocity: Māori Elderly and Whānau', *New Zealand Journal of Psychology*, 28:2 (1999) 101-106, pp. 101-102; p. 105.
25. Grace, *Chappy*, p. 13. Original emphasis.
26. Chadwick Allen, *Blood Narrative: Indigenous Identity in American Indian and Māori Literary and Activist Texts* (Durham: Duke UP, 2002), p. 128, pp. 132-6. Original emphasis.
27. Irene Visser, 'The Trauma of Goodness in Patricia Grace's Fiction', *The Contemporary Pacific*, 24:2 (2012) 279-321.
28. See Emily Kate Timms, '"Our Stories Could Kill You": Storytelling, Healthcare, and the Legacy of the "Talking Cure" in Patricia Grace's *Baby No-Eyes* (1998)' and Georgia Ka'apuni McMillen's *School for Hawaiian Girls* (2005)', *Journal of Postcolonial Writing*, 54:5 (2018) 627-40.
29. Grace, *Chappy*, p. 57.
30. Grace, *Chappy*, p. 57.
31. Poia Rewi, *Whaikorero: The World of Māori Oratory* (Auckland: Auckland UP, 2010), pp. 62-5.
32. Grace, *Chappy*, p. 57.
33. Grace, *Chappy*, p. 66.
34. Grace, *Chappy*, p. 70, p. 71.
35. Grace, *Chappy*, p. 104.
36. Grace, *Chappy*, p. 195.
37. Grace, *Chappy*, p. 197, p. 195.
38. Allen, *Blood Narrative*, p. 16, pp. 148-51.
39. Rebecca Wirihana and Cherryl Smith, 'Historical Trauma, Healing, and Well-being in Māori Communities', *MAI Journal*, 3.3 (2014) 197-210, p. 199.
40. Grace, *Chappy*, p. 198.
41. Grace, *Chappy*, p. 199.
42. Grace, *Chappy*, p. 202.
43. Elizabeth DeLoughrey, 'The Spiral Temporality of Patricia Grace's *Potiki*', *ARIEL: A Review of English Literature*, 30:1 (1999) 59-83, pp. 68-7, p. 99. Grace also draws heavily on Davianna Pōmaika'i McGregor's social and cultural history of Hawai'i. Davianna

Pōmaika'i McGregor, *Na Kua'aina: Living Hawaiian Culture* (Honolulu: U of Hawai'i P, 2007).

44. Grace, *Chappy*, p. 185.
45. Epeli Hau'ofa, 'The Ocean in Us', in *We Are the Ocean: Selected Works* (Honolulu: U of Hawai'i P, 2008), pp. 41-59, p. 51.
46. Grace, *Chappy*, p. 201.
47. Grace, *Chappy*, p. 202.
48. Grace, *Chappy*, p. 202.
49. Grace, *Chappy*, pp. 212-13.
50. Garett Kamemoto, 'Working Together for a Greater Wellbeing', *Ka Wai Ola*, 30:4 (2013) 18-19.
51. Ranginui Walker, *Ka Whawhai Tonu Matou: Struggle Without End* (Auckland: Penguin, 2004), pp. 12-15.
52. Grace, *Chappy*, p. 213.
53. Leonie John, '"i am the dreams of your tūpuna": Constructing Oceanic Memory in Contemporary Anglophone Māori Literature', *Pacific Dynamics: Journal of Interdisciplinary Research*, 2:2 (2018) 146-60, p. 152.
54. Grace, *Chappy*, p. 252.
55. Grace, *Chappy*, p. 252.

What Can We Learn from Stories of the Dying?: Narrative Extensions and the Absurdity of Being 'Terminal'

MICHELLE CHIANG

Death is a major and final life event. We do not know the exact time or under what circumstances it will happen but, like the birth of a new life, it too requires preparation. For the terminally ill, the time between the diagnosis and the inevitable is usually the period when preparation takes place, and those who write about this period often emphasize the importance of this preparatory experience. In the first of this two-part essay, with reference to the idea of the philosopher, Albert Camus, that humans exist in an absurd condition, I close read the temporal experiences articulated in the autobiographical narratives of Paul Kalanithi's *When Breath Becomes Air* and Georgia Blain's *The Museum of Words: a memoir of language, writing and mortality*. Through this, I identify the necessity of shifting from the perspective of time as quantifiable hours, minutes, and seconds that must be extended at all costs to a regard for time as qualitative moments to be lived intensely, doing what the dying deem is most important to them. In the second part, I posit that such a shift indicates that for persons who are not professional writers, early end-of-life conversations could facilitate the development of one's personal narrative and prepare one for the end. To understand the temporal experiences of an impending death is to understand the importance of regarding difficult end-of-life conversations as imperative conversations. Everyone, not just competent patients who are approaching the end of life, should be discussing and considering this life stage. More than just a chance to communicate how we would like to live out the rest of our days, such conversations are opportunities for personal growth as we develop our personal story while contemplating an 'absurd' predicament.

Dying is absurd

The 'absurd' is the 'confrontation between the human need [for reason] and the unreasonable silence of the world'.[1] Neither our inner longing for reason nor the external world's indifference to this need is absurd. Absurdity arises only when the two are placed together.[2] In the context of this essay, it is worth considering the terminally ill body as becoming part of the indifferent external world, since the diseased body becomes increasingly outside of our perceived control and unresponsive to our desire for it either to be well again or to offer a satisfactory answer to the questions 'why me?' and 'why now?' As such, it is not death but the process of dying from a terminal illness, when we are still able to question futilely and wonder persistently, which is absurd.

To elaborate let me draw upon three parables to situate the 'absurd'. First the Sisyphus story. While it is more usual to attend to the punishment Sisyphus incurred for tricking Thanatos and Persephone, that is to roll a giant boulder up a steep hill only to see it roll down again when it reaches the peak, I am concerned here with his death sentence for betraying Zeus as 'absurd'. Among many other more heinous crimes (murdering of travellers, plotting the downfall of his brother, impregnating his niece, causing the death of his sons borne by said niece), it is the seemingly innocuous deed of revealing to the river god, Aesopus, that Zeus has abducted his daughter Aegina, which leads to Sisyphus's condemnation by Zeus.[3] His death sentence should leave readers with many questions, such as why is Sisyphus punished for this deed but not for his more serious crimes, and why is telling the truth of an abduction a crime? But most readers don't question this since the tyrannical ego of Zeus, Supreme God and serial abductor, very likely plays a large part in the answers. Similarly, in the face of a terminal illness, any attempt to question why, for example, a malignant tumour would metastasize, and why one should have to suffer the punishing emotional and physical pain of an illness, would yield no meaningful answers. To understand what we can learn from narratives of the dying, I propose that we consider, first, that dying from a terminal illness is, in Camus's sense of the term, absurd, and writing about the dying experience articulates a 'definitive awakening' to this reality.[4]

My next parable comes from Camus's *L'Étranger*. In Stewart R. Sutherland's close reading of the novel in which the character, Meursault, is charged with a murder for which his motive remains unclear to the very end, he has it that the linear actions of Meursault leading to the murder are 'a set of connexions' that relate the character to the actual event, that is, the murder of the Arab.[5] Nevertheless, other than Meursault being the common denominator, these disjointed actions do not explain the murder. Simplistically interpreting the actions as connected in ways that could determine whether Meursault is a conventionally bad or good man, the prosecuting counsel makes Meursault out to be a cold-blooded murderer pursuing 'some sordid vendetta' whereas the defense counsel argues he is simply a grieving son who has lost his self-control.[6] Yet, by Meursault's account, he is neither of these. He killed a man 'because of the sun'.[7] My contention here is that absurdity arises as Camus insists upon the incommensurability between the counsels' and readers' search for a definitive murder motive in Meursault's set of tenuously related actions, and the actual crime which was triggered by 'the sun'. As such, Meursault's impending death as a result of his murder conviction is absurd. Attempts to question why he shot the Arab and how Meursault's death sentence fits a 'crime' without an established motive or intent would yield no satisfactory answer. Yet, Camus offers us the possibility of Meursault's happiness in the face of an absurd death sentence.

Instead of wallowing in misery as they confront their absurd predicaments, Sisyphus and Meursault are depicted as turning to possibilities that could bring them joy. Camus implores the reader to 'imagine Sisyphus happy' as he thinks of how '[e]ach atom of that stone, each mineral flake of that night-filled mountain, in itself forms a world' each time he walks down its slope to retrieve the boulder before resuming his climb up, and to picture Meursault happy as he waits for his death, fully conscious of his fate:[8]

> To feel [the benign indifference of the universe] so like myself, indeed, so brotherly, made me realize that I'd been happy, and that I was happy still. For all to be accomplished, for me to feel less lonely, all that remained to hope was that on the day of my execution there should be a huge crowd of spectators and that they should greet me with howls of execration.[9]

Camus's redirection of the reader to an alternate perspective in the face of an absurd predicament is not without precedent. In this – and I come here to my third and last parable – his Sisyphus and Meursault share a rebellious streak with Plato's Socrates. Charged with impiety and corrupting the minds of youth, instead of bargaining with the god of healing, Asclepius, for life, Socrates's final revolt within the absurdity of his death sentence, as depicted in Plato's *Phaedo*, is to remind Crito that 'we owe a cock to Asclepius. So pay the debt and don't be careless'.[10] William J. Gavin points out that '[m]ost commentators merely say that Asclepius was the god of healing and that in death Socrates is being cured from human ills' and they seem to neglect that 'most people would be bargaining with god(s) to let them live one more day. Socrates does the opposite'.[11] Persuasively, Colin Wells argues that the offering of the cock to the god of healing is to make up for the jailor's refusal to allow Socrates to pour a libation to the god before drinking the hemlock. Although upon the refusal, Socrates has immediately responded by praying without libation that 'my removal from this world to the other may be prosperous', his final instruction to Crito is really to discharge him from what he deems to be a debt for not pouring libation.[12] It is only in doing so, that Socrates can be assured he has created for himself the best chance of a 'prosperous' afterlife. Here, Socrates's investment in the possibility of an afterlife offers him an alternate perspective in the face of his death sentence. In the context of this essay, by rebelling *within* the confines of their absurd fates through the creation of alternate perspectives, Camus's Sisyphus and Meursault, Plato's Socrates, and the terminally ill memoirists share a narratological impulse to extend themselves beyond the absurd death sentence.

Narrative extensions

It is in the light of the possibilities of alternate stories as illustrated in the preceding section that I will now speak to the autobiographical experiences of Kalanithi and Blain, paying particular attention to the perspectives of time as represented in their aforementioned works. Central to the fact of dying, specifically from a terminal illness, the question which is generally posed is, 'What can the latest medical technology do to postpone death?' This question neglects the fact that the temporary postponement of death is the prolonging of the dying process. Since, as I assert, we experience time as both quantitative and qualitative, the fact of dying foregrounds the extension of quantitative time at the expense of qualitative time. On the one hand, quantitative time is understood as clock time, and it is defined by hours, minutes and seconds, with a perceived linearity from past, present, to future. Upon a terminal diagnosis, this perceived linearity is disrupted as one's future plans have to be put on hold or seem to fall apart completely. An instinctive desire to extend quantitative time is perfectly understandable. A large part of innovation and advancements in medical technology is driven by the impetus to prolong lives. Ideally, this would mean giving one a fighting chance to eventually regain the kind of life one would find meaningful, or just to live long enough to fulfil a lifelong dream. However, a focus on extending quantitative time could also lead to the acceptance of aggressive and/or experimental medical procedures that could prolong life but at a huge cost to the quality of life. The objective to stay alive at all costs may also lead to the demand for treatment without curative potential, extraordinary life-sustaining treatment which only prolongs the process of dying when death is imminent, and the delay or rejection of palliative care.

Qualitative time, on the other hand, is the experience of time in terms of its intensity. Kalanithi has it that

> The funny thing about time in the OR (Operating Room), whether you frenetically race or steadily proceed, is that you have no sense of it passing. If boredom is, as Heidegger argued, the awareness of time passing, this is the opposite. The intense focus makes the arms of the clock seem arbitrarily placed. Two hours can feel like a minute. Once the final stitch is placed and the wound is dressed, normal time suddenly restarts.[13]

We view quantitative clock time as 'normal time' and often neglect qualitative 'intensive time'. The insistence to stay alive at all costs is inextricably tied to the focus on time as quantitative, instead of it also being qualitative. Qualitative time, or intensive time, is nonlinear not because it eschews the temporal sequence of past, present, and future, but because it operates within the linear timeline by highlighting events that matter to the individual who experienced and is experiencing them, with or without regard for chronology, and ties them up into a personal narrative, understood within the self as a single complex whole.

Such events in the personal narrative are often those that mark one's roles as, for example, a daughter/son, spouse, parent or sibling. They are non-linear and constituted by everything that make one's life meaningful. The dangers of fixating on extending one's quantitative time include pushing qualitative time to the background of our minds, and neglecting to live intensely. Quality of life for the terminally ill is the extent an individual remains connected with the roles one played before the terminal diagnosis, and the extent one retains the capacity to perform tasks that are important to them, such as keeping oneself clean and presentable to others, communicating with loved ones, or being able to stay at the job one loves. Quality of life can therefore be understood as the extent to which one remains connected with the shaping and reshaping of a life story. It is in this engagement with the personal narrative that the memoirs of Kalanithi and Blain demonstrate a crucial shift from the initial perception of time as a disrupted linearity, to a qualitative experience as the writers round out the personal story, and bring focus back to what is most important and meaningful to the individual, in the face of a terminal illness.

In their deep engagement with the subject, Kalanithi and Blain do not write about their dying experience as heroic quests, but as a turn to the imagination and memory to extend their narratives beyond their absurd predicaments. In *When Breath Becomes Air*, Kalanithi turns his attention from his impending death to the impending birth of his daughter to contemplate how he could make the most of his relationship with her within and beyond the brief period of time he has. Central to *The Museum of Words* are Blain's intergenerational relationships with her mother, her best friend, and her daughter that shaped her identity as a writer whose words will live through her loved ones and her readers. Living within the absurdity of the Camusean death sentence, both memoirists turn their attention to the relationships that matter most in the present and would almost certainly outlast the ailing body to continue extending into the future through another. Such a projection into the future, is a revolt within the absurd predicament, to extend their personal narratives beyond their death sentences.

At the start of his memoir, Kalanithi points out he had pursued medicine 'to bear witness to the twinned mysteries of death, its experiential and biological manifestations: at once deeply personal and utterly impersonal'.[14] As a patient, the writer would go beyond witnessing, to experience and share with his readers his dying as a deeply personal *and* impersonal process. Death may not have subjective meaning, but as long as we are still breathing, his memoir teaches us, meaning can be generated for the self and others through words. Similarly Blain, whose condition involves a tumour sitting in the language centre of her brain, is a professional writer who faces increasing difficulties doing what she loves but perseveres anyway, to go beyond the tale of

> how most illness memoirs go – you fall ill, you prove your heroic qualities in the face of this challenge, you are treated and do battle with the illness, and the sickness is defeated, or you are defeated, but you have learnt what it is to live, and you have made peace with yourself and those around you. I don't want to tell this tale.[15]

In Kalanithi and Blain's memoirs, their narratives attend to alternate possibilities of telling their stories within the Camusean death sentence. What lies at the heart of the memoirs is a subjectivity which engages with the imagination to generate a myriad of perspectives about living and dying. These perspectives are created not from their illnesses but from a reality altered by their terminal illnesses. Blain tells us the story of Princess Scheherazade, who survives her marriage to the murderous King Shahryar by telling him a story every night for one thousand and one nights until he eventually falls in love with her and she is safe from the death sentence that befell the wives before her. Blain imagines herself like Scheherazade and wonders if she too could live to see another day as long as she keeps telling stories about her life.[16] In many ways, memoirs that attend to alternate stories within the experience of one's terminal illness seem to employ a frame narrative technique where the main narrative is the illness event and a set of smaller narratives are generated around it, then embedded within it. Essentially, the embedded stories create multiple perspectives from which to broach a personal reality that has been altered by terminal illness.

Anne Jurecic highlights the difficulty of this creative process: 'Those who write about illness, an experience that can break a life in two, face the nearly impossible task that confronts all who write about trauma: how to speak the unspeakable.'[17] Waking up in pain and facing another day, Kalanithi takes comfort in the closing words of *The Unnamable* by the absurdist writer, Samuel Beckett, 'I can't go on. I'll go on.'[18] The lived experience of illness demands to be articulated in language even if it defies discursivity. James E. Pennebaker suggests that writing about traumatic experiences could allow one to gain insight at a time of uncertainty, and Mike Bury points out that '[n]ot only do language and narrative help sustain and create the fabric of everyday life, they feature prominently in the repair and restoring of meanings when they are threatened'.[19] Moreover, writing about illness is an empowering way to reclaim the patient's voice. Brian Hurwitz and Victoria Bates observe that

> The passivity that so frequently accompanies severe illness is made all the more profound as a result of the language to which patienthood is subjected by modern healthcare, which has been colonized by objectivist interests and concepts that threaten to eclipse the communal language of the lifeworld, the everyday concerns of bodily and psychic experience.'[20]

Arthur W. Frank uses the metaphor of colonization too when he compares the diseased body to a geographic territory 'on which a foreign power – medicine – plants its flag and claims governing prerogatives, disregarding those who were already there'.[21] Therefore, despite the difficulty, it is imperative to continue narrating and developing the personal story, 'to speak for oneself about how to be ill, rather than being spoken by institutional discourses'.[22]

So what is the takeaway from Kalanithi and Blain's memoirs for those who are not professional writers and who do not know how to begin preparing for the end? This is the main concern in the question in the title of this essay and it is elucidated in the section which follows. Memoirs of the dying, as noted above, are more than heroic quests to overcome the challenges which a terminal illness has thrown at the authors and their loved ones. The narratives of Kalanithi and Blain are prime examples of self-advocation and the refusal to let the struggle to gain another quantifiable day get in the way of developing their personal stories to the very end. With this understanding I shall now take a closer look at end-of-life conversations, specifically focusing on how it could support personal narrative development, not only for non-professional writers facing the end of life, but also for those who are still healthy.

Developing the personal narrative through end-of-life conversations

End-of-life conversations include a wide range of topics from treatment choices to concerns about coping with the foreclosure of a life. Dale G. Larson and Daniel R. Tobin point out that 'when these often difficult discussions are avoided or are managed poorly, the quality of remaining life for patients can be seriously jeopardized'.[23] In the context of a terminal illness, avoiding end-of-life conversations could mean perpetuating patients' binary thinking as they consider whether they should try to live at all costs or give up completely. It also leaves the healthcare professionals' false dichotomy unchecked as they decide whether a terminally ill patient should be treated for certain medical conditions. As Stuart J. Youngner and Jerry M. Shuck observe, '[p]atients, families, and health professionals tend to conceptualize treatment limitation dichotomously – either we go all out to save the patient or we let the patient die'.[24] Avoiding this false dichotomy involves asking and answering difficult questions about what quality of life means to the patient, and the degree of invasive treatment one is willing to accept to achieve such a quality of life. Going beyond binary thinking, questions on treatment limitations and goals could potentially save patients from overtreatment, and allow them to consider alternate possibilities regarding how they would like to live out the rest of their lives.

Highlighting that, as numerous studies reveal, the lack of timely and effective end-of-life discussions have resulted in patients dying from unrelieved pain due to prolonged hospitalization or intensive care, Larson and Tobin suggest that the barriers to end-of-life conversations can be overcome by building better interpersonal communication skills in clinicians, adopting a patient-centred model of care, putting focus on the patient's quality of life by the medical team, and facilitating discussions earlier in the healthcare process. I would like to discuss further the urgency of the last suggestion but, first, it is important that we recognize these possible solutions to improve the quality of end-of-life conversations emphasize what healthcare professionals can do for the patients, while patients continue to be sidelined in passive roles as potential receivers of improved care. Larson and Tobin's report is now almost two decades old, and healthcare professionals today continue to grapple with the barriers to end-of-life conversations observed in that report.[25] I think a missing piece of the proposed solution is awareness. That is, I assert that just as it is crucial for clinicians to understand that through end-of-life conversations the personal narrative can continue to develop and grow during life's final stage, the layperson (not just patients) should be aware that they too can benefit from engaging in end-of-life conversations.

Initiatives such as Michelle Winslow's Oral History Service at Sheffield, which has now expanded to five services in the north of England and Northern Ireland, involves sitting with the terminally ill patient, with a recorder, and letting him or her 'talk about whatever you want to talk about' and 'for as long as you like'.[26] A qualitative research to assess the impact of recording the oral history of patients in palliative care yielded excellent results in which both patients and bereaved relatives find the service and recording cathartic. Winslow and Sam Smith concluded that this catharsis is afforded by the 'opportunities to talk about their past and present in a non-medical context'.[27] Winslow's work attests to the importance of the personal narrative to patients as they face their absurd predicament, and also to the bereaved who upon receiving the recordings hold in their hands an extension of the departed beyond death. More crucially, Winslow's research and service highlight that end-of-life conversations do not have to be directly related to a medical context. For those who are still healthy, conversations based on a hypothetical illness or death afford us the opportunities to develop the personal narrative by leading us to a clearer idea of what is most important and meaningful to us in this life.

To begin an end-of-life conversation with loved ones, one could consider asking two questions: 'Who are the people and what are the things that are most important to me?' and 'How would a debilitating illness affect my relationship with these people and things?' In interviews and accounts recorded in Ira Byock's seminal work *Dying Well: Peace and Possibilities at the End of Life*, we learn that answers to these questions do not have to be extremely profound to have significant impact on an individual's quality of life at the end of life. For example, to Anne-Marie Wilson it was important that she improved her relationship with her daughter, and should she lose the capacity to speak or care for herself, she would like her caregivers to know she did not want to have pain and did not want to smell bad. Between her cancer diagnosis and her eventual death from the illness, she attended her daughter's wedding which 'represented [to her] an opportunity to fulfil her role as [a] mother. ... After the wedding, she told herself, there would be fewer loose ends'.[28] When she slipped into a coma, her loved ones and healthcare team took extra care to honour her wishes and tried their best to reduce her pain and ensure that she did not smell bad. This example demonstrates that considering and conveying to our loved ones what is most important to us not only brings to the foreground of our consciousness the people and activities that are meaningful and important, it helps caregivers to know how best to care for us when our capacity to advocate for the self becomes significantly diminished. This leads us back to the urgency of having end-of-life discussions early.

In a recent article by Rebecca Voelker on the launch of more initiatives to raise public awareness about the importance of having end-of-life conversations, a healthcare professional R. Sean Morrison observes,

> [L]ook at the people who were attending the Death Cafes; it's not the folks who are living with cancer... it's not the folks living with advanced heart failure. It's healthy, young and middle-aged folks who are getting together to talk about something very, very hypothetical.[29]

He adds that '[a]ll the opinions, thoughts, and ideas expressed during those conversations "will go away when it's really you"'.[30] What seems to be overlooked by Morrison and those who agree with him that end-of-life discussions are too hypothetical without the onset of disease, is the critical objective of such community outreach projects to help people overcome the discomfort of talking about dying. When people are uncomfortable talking about death and dying, a barrier to self-advocacy is erected and '[l]acking a coherent view of how people might live successfully all the way to their very end, we [allow] our fates to be controlled by the imperatives of medicine, technology, and strangers'.[31] The term 'end-of-life' denotes the subject of the conversation, but the conversation does not have to happen only as we are months or weeks away from death. We should understand these conversations as imperative conversations that should occur throughout our lives to avoid letting the imperatives of medicine, technology, and strangers take control over our personal story if or when the unexpected happens.

We have learnt from stories of the dying that words extend the personal narrative beyond the authors' absurd death sentences to generate meaning for themselves while they are alive, and for the reader even when they are gone. For non-professional writers, conversations with loved ones about dying, which should begin when one is still capable of making decisions, can help us reorganize the personal narrative, generate personal meaning and better prepare us for death too. End-of-life conversations that occur in a medical setting usually entail the stating of end-of-life preferences in Advanced Care Plans (ACP), Preferred-Plan-of-Care (PPC) or Advanced Care Directives (ACD). These conversations involve the sharing of personal values and beliefs that are to a large extent directly related to healthcare preferences under different medical circumstances. But end-of-life conversations that take place earlier while one is still healthy allow us to develop our personal narrative in tandem with acquiring new knowledge about how others are able to 'leave well' through the exchange of information with friends and family, as well as through participating in community initiatives to learn more about making care decisions. There are not many who can articulate as well as Kalanithi and Blain the development of the personal narrative in the face of an absurd predicament, but, like them, we possess a personal story which, through early end-of-life conversations with our loved ones, can continuously evolve, generate meaning and extend beyond a current narrative of the self.

NOTES

1. Albert Camus, *The Myth of Sisyphus*, trans. Justin O'Brien (London: Penguin Books, 2000), p. 31.
2. Camus, *The Myth of Sisyphus*, p. 34.
3. Elliott M. Simon, *The Myth of Sisyphus: Renaissance Theories of Human Perfectibility* (Madison: Fairleigh Dickinson UP, 2007), p. 29.
4. Camus, *The Myth of Sisyphus*, p. 19.
5. Stewart R. Sutherland, 'Imagination in Literature and Philosophy: A Viewpoint in Camus's *L'étranger*', *The British Journal of Aesthetics*, 10:3 (1970) 268-9.
6. Albert Camus, *The Stranger*, trans., Stuart Gilbert (New York: Vintage Books, 1942), p. 60.
7. Camus, *The Stranger*, p. 64.
8. Camus, *The Myth of Sisyphus*, p. 19.
9. Camus, *The Stranger*, p. 76.
10. Plato, *Phaedo* (Indiana: Hackett Publishing, 1998), p. 101.
11. William J. Gavin, 'Plato: On Death and Dying', *Journal of Thought*, 9:4 (1974) 240.
12. Colin Wells, 'The Mystery of Socrates' Last Words', *Arion: A Journal of Humanities and the Classics* (Fall 2008) 141.
13. Paul Kalanithi, *When Breath Becomes Air* (New York: Random House, 2016), p. 104, Kindle edition.
14. Kalanithi, *When Breath Becomes Air*, p. 53.
15. Georgia Blain, *The Museum of Words: a memoir of language, writing and mortality* (Victoria,

Vic.: Scribe Publications, 2017), p. 139.

16. Blain, *The Museum of Words*, p. 102.

17. Anne Jurecic, *Illness as Narrative* (Pittsburgh: U of Pittsburgh P, 2012), p. 10.

18. Kalanithi, *When Breath Becomes Air*, p. 149.

19. Mike Bury, 'Illness narratives: fact of fiction', *Sociology of Health and Illness*, 23:3 (2001) 263-85, p. 264.

20. Brian Hurwitz and Victoria Bates, 'The Roots and Ramifications of Narrative in Modern Medicine', in *The Edinburgh companion to the critical medical humanities* (Edinburgh: Edinburgh UP, 2016), pp. 559-76 (568).

21. Arthur W. Frank, 'From sick role to narrative subject: An analytic memoir', *Health*, 20:1 (2016) 9-21. p. 11.

22. Frank, 'From sick role to narrative subject, p. 10.

23. Dale G. Larson and Daniel R. Tobin, 'End-of-Life Conversations: Evolving Practice and Theory', *JAMA*, 284:12 (2000) 1573-8, p. 1573.

24. Stuart J. Youngner and Jerry M. Shuck, 'Advance Directives and the Determination of Death', in *Surgical Ethics*, eds, Laurence B. McCullough, James W. Jones and Baruch A. Brody (New York: Oxford UP, 1998), p. 64.

25. See Sarah Bessen et. al, '"Sharing in hopes and worries" - a qualitative analysis of the delivery of compassionate care in palliative care and oncology at end of life', *International Journal of Qualitative Studies on Health and Well-being*, 14:1 (2019). Doi: 10.1080/17482631.2019.1622355.

26. 'Interview with Michelle Winslow and Sam Smith', *Medical Humanities at the University of Sheffield*, 25 June 2014.

27. Michelle Winslow, Sam Smith, 'How does providing an oral history at the end of life influence well-being of the individual and the bereaved?' *BMJ Supportive & Palliative Care*, 2014; 4: A16.

28. Ira Byock, *Dying Well: Peace and Possibilities at the End of Life* (New York: Riverhead books, 1997), p. 46.

29. R. Sean Morrison, quoted in Rebecca Voelker, 'Building a Better Death, One Conversation at a Time', *JAMA*, 322:3 (June 2019) 195-7, pp. 196-7.

30. Morrison, quoted in Voelker, 'Building a Better Death', p. 197.

31. Atul Gawande, *Being Mortal: Medicine and What Matters in the End* (New York: Picador, 2014), p. 9.

Four Steps to Immunity

Step 1: Foreign bodies (pathogens) invade the body. These pathogens have antigens on their surface that are entirely unique to them.

"Quick! pull her up! Underneath, underneath her arm Nilo. Rukhsana! Rukhsana come here we need you! Rukhsana come out! Amma? Amma are you OK amma?"

A single groan, when enunciated with controlled precision, is enough to unleash an Armageddon from within these walls. The sun, for Imy, lies fallen out of the sky sitting crashed at the bottom of the stairs. Having attempted to crane over this motionless hulk beached across the bathroom tiles, Nilo eventually releases her stretched sinewed arms, walking across the bathroom to blow into some toilet roll.

"Nilo! Nilo come on let's try again!" Imy catches his reflection in the mirror beside Nilo, his pleading wallowed face side by side against Nilo's ethereal stare. He knows that stare too well. He knows the cogs behind it and the thoughts it moulds. Though yet unvoiced, he feels its scream.

"Rukhsana! Arre, where are you, are you deaf?"

A single wince shudders across Amma's form like a wave; the tremors that herald an earthquake.

"Rukhsana! For God's sake quick!"

A door eventually swings open to reveal the T-shirt and jogging bottomed outline of Rukhsana. The sounds of children play-fighting echo from behind her. A cough ricochets out as she walks, her quickening motion building concern with each step.

"Amma's been on the floor like this and I've been calling you for hours. Are you deaf in there?"

Rukhsana kneels at her mother's head, caressing Amma's forehead with gentle hands, *"Amma! Don't worry I'm here OK"*

"Are you listening?" demands Imy. *"I said where were you?"*

"Do you really think Amma needs this?" Rukhsana replies.

"Now you're going to tell me what Amma needs?"

Another wince, another groan, and attention is rightfully restored to where it should be.

Nilo re-emerges from between the siblings. "*We'll both grab her right arm Rukhsana.*" Imy stands hooking his arm on the other side. "*One-two-three!*" Back first, Amma concertinas up to her knees, bones clicking as she does. A sigh just short of loud and a grimace just squeezed from a scream work collectively as though absorbing a thousand wounds.

Imy calls down, "*Amma you OK?*" She nods. Once.

"*Amma don't worry OK Amma. We're here,*" affirms Rukhsana.

"*One more time, to her feet.*"

Nilo leads, causing the mighty Amma to rise lopsidedly like a camel. The siblings follow Nilo's lead as she heads the march into Amma's room, sitting her upon the bed.

"*You OK?*" Nilo asks curtly.

Amma winces, collapsing her head onto her knees, conveniently, in the direction of her dutiful son.

"*Where does it hurt Amma? Hmm? Tell me. Here? Your knees? Does this hurt?*"

"*Of course it hurts stop doing it to her,*" Rukhsana snaps at her brother. "*Amma I'll get hot milk and turmeric for you yeah? Just wait here. I'll get the hot milk and turmeric for you Amma.*"

"*Wait, I'll get it. Honey! I'll put honey too.*"

With Imy out of the room Rukhsana reaches across Amma's bedside table for a pungent balm. Carefully peeling up her shalwar she exposes a dot-to-dot canvas of markings collected by her advancing years. Rukhsana treats each one as though they were immovable scars of anguish. Each familiar with this ritual, every application is echoed with simultaneous intakes of sharp breath between mother and daughter.

"*Why you haven't you brushed your hair Rukhsana? It's half the day gone already.*"

Rukhsana's silence aptly conveys the full volume of her suffering while Nilo stands apart looking on and looking through this exhibition of filial piety. Imy arrives and immediately takes Amma's face into one hand whilst carefully delivering his prepared concoction with the other, thus also making known his part in her servitude. All the while he pretends Nilo isn't looking through them, hoping if he doesn't look he won't see.

Allowing what's carrying on to carry on Nilo takes gentle steps out of the room and through the shadowed corridor with almost all the doors shut to her. Feeling nodules in the carpet below her feet she wonders when they appeared. The door to Rukhsana's room at the end is still open. Her two sons Umar and Bilal play on their playstation from the bottom bunk of their beds. Duvets are thrown on the floor, clothes on beds, plates on TVs, on chest of drawers, on threadbare carpets. This was once meant to be a nursery. To imagine anything else there now the entire walls would have to be re-plastered. Gliding down the stairs, scratches graze her palm on the banister beneath it and words she's never uttered are scrawled across the walls.

She fixes for herself a cup of hot milk with turmeric in the microwave. A remedial elixir as old as dusty Indian villages is these days nuked into convenient existence. Trendy people drink it in trendy cafes giving it a trendy name – Golden Milk. For Nilo it's difficult to reconcile trendiness with the stench of being mildly diseased and Indian. She blows into a kitchen roll watching her cup orbit through galaxies of appropriation.

Closing the last door of the house behind her, she steps out into her garden. Her runner beans have obediently caught grip of the canes she placed in their pots. The lavender has already outgrown itself; bees weave in and out of them. She catches sight of her first butterfly of the year. It flits in over the fence but then as though startled to find itself here, flits right back again over again. Here is her defence.

Hidden among the lavender are her emergency cigarettes, only two left. Avoiding the bees she retrieves a small plastic bag containing her box and lighter. Golden milk in one hand and Marlboro Light in the other, Nilo takes deliberate inhalations vividly picturing silken-grey plumes swirling about her lungs before released as clouds leaving tenacious threads that linger in her innermost lungs, her throat, around the base of her tongue. Looking into the kitchen window she catches her own faint reflection. Her lips seem thinner now. Full lips are quite popular these days. People are having bits taken out of other bits of their bodies just to make their lips fuller. It's a thing apparently.

"You've got a cold."

Imy's arrival the other side of the window doesn't startle Nilo. There are days when his absence is as inconsequential as his presence.

"You shouldn't be smoking with a cold."

She takes a sip of her turmeric milk, imagining any remnants of smoke still clinging to the inside of her throat being washed into her stomach by a thick golden waterfall.

"You're annoyed." Smoke fills the space where a response should be. *"I always know when you're annoyed. You won't admit it but I know you are. It would help you if you'd at least admit it. At least say you're annoyed. You think it's not obvious? Everyone knows you know. Everyone can see it."*

Some stories seem too cumbersome to begin again. Nilo is already way in so why should she have to relive the beginning again, just because he was blind to it the first time. Retelling the start of any story midway is always so boring.

"*She's my mother. I can't change that.*"

Imy fires a range of attempts that might force a response.

"*Why are you making me feel like I'm doing something wrong by looking after her? That's exactly what you're doing you know. And stop blowing smoke at me when I'm trying to talk to you!*"

"*It's the wind.*"

"*I see. You want to drag this out. Punish me until I say the right thing. I didn't know you wanted turmeric milk too. You don't think I'd have made you one as well if I'd have known? God! Do you not think the day's been bad enough already?*"

"*She didn't fall so bad.*"

"*Are you even listening to yourself? Fear God if nothing else, that's an infirm woman you're talking about not least my mother! I...I've tried. I've tried talking to you. The rest, the rest is up to you now!*"

Step 2: A range of lymphocytes from within the bloodstream attempt to counter the pathogen until an appropriate lymphocyte is activated. Antibodies are secreted that fit the specific antigens of the pathogens.

Initially it's a paste. Water needs to be added slowly, sparingly, ensuring all the flour is caught and brought together into the emulsion. It doesn't take long before it starts to collect and bind, becoming firmer with each action. Initially it's the fingers that swirl, then the base of the palm and finally the fists that work themselves into it before a uniform mound is created: soft, flawless, firm. Upon pressing it should rise back to regain its original position. Lentils simmer on the hob voraciously sucking up as much water as you care to deliver them. Like a mad scientist's experiment, bubbled webbing sporadically creeps from under the lid, knocking it from side to side, fragrant steam filling every corner, every nook.

Her fist is locked deep in the dough now and next to this strange coagulation, her skin appears only a few shades darker. It didn't use to be, before. Before she ever needed to make dough. She takes a finger from her free hand and repeatedly jabs into both. Sometimes her skin rises back quicker, sometimes the dough. Some women even have stuff injected into their faces. Apparently that's a thing too, just like with the lips. Bits injected out of other parts of the body, re-injected into their faces. She wishes she knew how quickly her skin should bounce back, she'd never timed it at eighteen or twenty-one or even at twenty-seven. She'd never thought it could be important to know one day. She'd probably never imagined her skin to be anything but firm, her hair to be anything but full, her smile anything but easy.

As easy as he appeared to be when they first met, strolling across Leicester Square to speak to her with his friends glaring in shock and envy from the other side of the square, jostling to steal glances between the rushing hoards.

"You stood out to me in the middle of these thousands of people. I had to come over and say hello."

He was completely at ease with his audacity. She remembers catching her reflection in his sunglasses, embarrassed by the fullness of her own smile. She remembers how sharp, how well groomed he was. She liked his height and toned shoulders, his sleek neck. She was so overcome at the thought of having been noticed in the middle of so many people, she never even wondered what his friends were laughing about at the other end, how many times they'd done this already that day, or for how many days, how many times he might have said those same words. She squints into her memory to see if she might tell how firm her skin was then, or how full her lips.

It's all coming from their butts apparently, their behinds. All this extra fullness and firmness is derived from a person's own backside to be rehabitated wherever appears most deflated at the time. Is she the only one anymore to whom it seems disturbing, disgusting even, that one's own behind, the most hidden of nether regions, could now take pride of place on one's own face? Who could have thought that the bottom, its multiple names that for so long have been either a source of laughter or abuse, should today be the font from which eternal beauty is sought?

And what when the behind is itself the area of need, because that too is a thing now right – the round, elevated posterior? What when the source requires replenishment? From where is this need delivered? Another posterior perhaps, one packed with an excess enabling beauty to travel as though a currency perfectly redistributing itself wherever the need be greatest.

At which point exactly did she lose it? Perhaps, unbeknown to her, it was that first encounter in Leicester Square, snared as she was amid those thousand others, her beauty devoured by laughing hyenas. Or perhaps it was later, as they began to relax around one another, it could have been at the very point of relaxing? Or their wedding, under the gaze of so many – perhaps a drop was sucked out by each gaze while she froze under flashing lights. Was it the anxiety of blank walls in their new home, or the resentment at having them filled by others? Perhaps it was all of it. And now she was left somewhat less, less defined, less taut, just less.

She raised her fist out from the dough and stood over the sink to cough when Bilal, Rukhsana's ten-year-old son, charged into the kitchen.

"*I want water mami.*"

"*What do you say?*"

"*Please!*"

He gulps down the water she gives him so fast it spills down his front leaving a tiny puddle at his feet.

"*What you doing Nilo mami?*"

"*I'm cooking. What you doing?*"

"*I'm drinking water.*"

"*And what you doing after drinking water?*"

"*I don't know. I've finished my game and Tariq's annoying me. Can I help you cook?*"

"*I didn't know you liked to cook. What do you cook?*"

"*I used to make toast with butter and jam and once I helped my mum make scrambled eggs, I did the whisking and I'm really good at opening boiled eggs.*"

"*Wow! A proper little Masterchef, why don't you help me roll some chapattis?*"

"*Cool! From the dough with the stick? Yeah come on!*"

Nilo breaks out perfectly spherical dough-balls from within her palms and Bilal immediately sets to work on them, rolling out every deviation from a circle that's possible. Africa, South-America, the USA, each outline of a new continent causing them to erupt into laughter together.

"*You don't worry Billy! They're each beautiful and they'll be just delicious too. We'll save these ones for me and you later.*"

"*No I like your chapattis, your cooking is always the best. You're nice. Me and Tariq said the other day. You're nice, that's why your food is the nicest.*"

"*And I'm round so my chapattis are too?*"

"*You're not round. You're straight.*"

"*Bilal! What you doing down here?*" Rukhsana has made her way down as far as the kitchen, a rare sighting. "*I told you you're not supposed to be in the kitchen. It's not good for your asthma!*"

"*Look Amma I made America!*"

"*Get upstairs now!*"

Nilo gives the boy a little nod and a smile. He strops his way upstairs.

"*Rukhsana give us a hand making these.*"

"*Huh? Oh erm. I really, you know, I really would if I could Nilo but you just can't understand. Trust me, even just being here right now, talking to you. It's a lot. It really is a lot for me right now. What can I tell you? I just wouldn't wish this*" on anyone. Not my enemies. Every day I ask myself you know? How did it end up like this? Why did we marry, why I put up with it all? Why didn't he ever treat me like I deserved to be treated? Do you know the taunts my children have suffered at school! He should at least have spent on his children if not me."

"It's OK. I'll do it".

"It's best anyway, kitchen's so small we'd just get in each other's way. How's your cold, flu, virus thing? Still have it? I hope Bilal doesn't get it. He just shook one off."

"We got it off Bilal."

"Give us a shout when it's done huh? Amma's hungry too."

Nilo stares into the mound of dough and uncooked chapattis. Coughing she steps away and walks to look out of the window while blowing her nose. Her garden was just a yard when they first acquired it, the floor concreted over, dark fencing constantly on the verge of collapse. She'd tended to it so carefully. The lavender was carefully placed so as to guide the eye around the space. In the spring and summer the breezes carries the scent inside. Runner beans replace potatoes each alternate year and sit in between, providing food and flowers. In front of everything sit a series of smaller pots of sweet peas, pansies and geraniums – vivid brushstrokes of colour. Bees come to her garden for the lavender, other smaller insects appear like flying specks. There are moths and flies and blue bottles, she's even seen a dragonfly. The right insects cross-pollinate her runners and she gets beans. She longs for butterflies that eat the parasites that do nothing but feed upon what she's created. There's a whole ecosystem she's created, an oasis amidst concrete yards and parking spaces; everything playing its own specific role in keeping the whole system balanced.

She looks on at a system of which she too is a part. It is her design after all, her pruning, her digging and her tending that's made this – her beauty. Locked in this thought her eyes are forced into focus by a white blur shocking her sightline. A butterfly, cabbage-white, flying towards her sits the other side of the window perfectly still, a mere breath away from her. Then another. Then three and four and then five cabbage-white butterflies sit the other side of the window. There've never been so many as five at one time before, her meagre garden had never attracted so many. She'd never thought it could. And just as suddenly they disappeared, punctuating that last thought.

Step 3: The activated lymphocytes divide over and over to produce clones of identical lymphocytes.

Nilo immediately switches off all the hobs on the cooker. The dough is left unrolled, chapattis left uncooked, daal left unsatiated. She storms up the stairs and slams open Rukhsana's door.

"I'm not going to do it anymore. If you want some food, you'll have to make it."

Released, she charges into her room, her bedroom overlooking the garden. She can see the bees, other hovering insects. There are no butterflies anymore. She can see no more butterflies. There are no fields or meadows around here. Just rows upon rows of houses, shops and garages. There's probably not another butterfly for miles.

"Nilo I don't know what you think you're doing charging into our room and shouting at me and my children like that! Do you think I can't make a meal? Do you think we're all just sat around dependent on you to eat!"

Sniffling, Nilo locks the door to her room from inside. Muffled echoes continue.

"How can…Amma…ill…selfish…Imy…work…children…"

She sits at her chair in front of the dresser. She hasn't done this for a while. She hasn't sat face to face with herself for some time, her back upright, neck tall again. On the dresser is a picture of herself and Imy at their wedding. There's another from a year later when they went to Sharm-el-Sheikh, just the two of them. She compares her shoulders now to then – perhaps not as straight, but they still seem much the same: long and slender. Her skin – it's difficult to say whether it's the same firmness just from a picture, besides she's smiling in the picture. The face changes completely when you smile. She tries. It feels strange, forced. She tries again, stretching it further but that only exaggerates the falseness of it. She looks out at her garden and imagines when they first moved in, Imy placing the pots around exactly where she wanted them, her arms deep in the soil, Imy standing in the doorway with hot cups of tea. She looks in the mirror again, opens her hair and smiles. Her eyes big, sharp, sparkling. Her cheeks high, teeth bright, lips alive.

She pauses, shaken by herself. She hadn't seen herself like this before. Yes there are the beginnings of lines around her smile that she'd never seen before but she likes them. She likes everything. She looks good. She looks good even compared to her past pictures, she looks good compared to how she remembered herself, she looks good even compared to that twenty-something receptionist Imy couldn't stop staring at yesterday at the doctor's. She is beautiful.

"Nilo! Nilo! Rukhsana knocks on her door as though to break through it. *What you doing Nilo? Amma's not well she needs food. Don't be concerned about me or little Bilal and Tariq but at least Amma? She's old Nilo! Nilo are you listening?"*

She loves her hair. She loves it more than anyone else's. She loves it more than the receptionist's. She loves how her skin has allowed her smile to expand, not constrict. She loves this new look in her eyes. She's not been able to just look at herself for so long.

"Nilo! Have you become mad? What are you doing, get out! Amma look! Look what's happened to your daughter-in-law, look. See what she's doing. We're too much for her can you see? A little chapatti and daal even has become too much for her!"

A haze catches the corner of Nilo's eye; scores of white butterflies, hundreds, possibly more all heading towards her garden. From some indecipherable place a whole cloud dances through the air towards her.

Step 4. Each cloned lymphocyte releases antibodies that collectively succeed in destroying pathogens. Bacteria in particular are devoured though the process of Phagocytosis. Once the pathogens have been destroyed the lymphocytes are mostly broken down, though some remain in the bloodstream. These are called memory lymphocytes.

"Nilo open this door it's me!"

Imy's bass-pitched urgency travels straight through the door. Nilo calmly walks over.

"Nilo it's me. Open this…"

"Salaam."

"Walaikum salaam. What's Rukhsana saying Nilo?"

"What's she saying? I've not been listening."

"She's saying you're refusing to give them food?"

"That's not true. I just wasn't going to cook today."

"Nilo. You know the situation. You know Amma can hardly move and…"

"… Rukhsana can."

"Nilo she's going through a hard time. Nilo I thought you understood."

Rukhsana appears from behind her brother.

"You've no need to intercede with your wife on my behalf. I know it's the sight of me and my children she can't stand! This is my brother's home do you understand, I'm no stranger here! You lot bought it with the inheritance my dad left you. I've just as much right to be here as anyone. More right than you even. You listening? If it wasn't for my dad you'd have none of this."

"What do you mean your dad. Wasn't he my dad too? And so what if I bought this..."

Nilo is still fixated upon that incoming cloud. Letting the screaming talk to itself, she steps past them both like a ghost, descending down the stairs and back into the kitchen, now darkened by an entire blanket of white butterflies fluttering their wings upon brick and glass as though attempting to break through. Nilo stands frozen.

Upstairs the familiar sounds ricochet between walls and corridors.

"Have you heard this Amma? We're not wanted here anymore Amma. We're being made homeless! I should never have come here, we should never have come here!"

"Rukhsana stop spewing your vile poison!"

"Oh I'm the one with the vile poison am I? You and your delicate little wifey are made of pure snow I suppose!"

"I've had it up to here with you, all of you! All I've tried is to just maintain some sense of us being a family for God's sake...Nilo!"

Imy charges down the stairs.

"Nilo where the heck are..."

Imy too froze at the bottom of the stairs. Words continued being thrown around above them as husband and wife both stood like statues.

"Selfish...should never have...shame...community...streets..."

"What's going on Nilo? What is this?"

Nilo turns her head to look straight at Imy.

"I'm still beautiful Imy. Do you know that?"

"What? What are you saying?"

Nilo walks over to the door.

"Nilo what are you doing? Are you mad? Don't open the door to them we need to call the RSPCA or something."

"Married her...mistake...family...different...arrogant...one chapatti."

Nilo opens the door. Like a plague the cloud rushes into her home. Leaving Nilo and Imy untouched they swarm upstairs together in a perfectly synchronised dance of devastation, descending upon each unknown, each foreign body, each parasite.

Imy screams his way through the dark fog, as they flit in vengeful fury against his face as he attempts a passage through them. His arms raised in front of his face desperate to create an opening, he falls down to his knees and screams for Amma to be OK.

Nilo remains at the doorway. Nothing can be done now. Each must play its own specific role in keeping the whole system balanced.

Biocolonial Fictions: Medical Ethics and New Extinction Discourse in Contemporary Biopiracy Narratives

CLARE BARKER

The age of big pharma, population genetics, and global health initiatives that transcend national borders has ushered in new forms of extractivism that consist of mining the bodies of Indigenous people, their medicinal plants, and their traditional ecological knowledge (TEK) for their pharmacological potential. These new forms of scientific endeavour echo and reconfigure the colonialist appropriations of the past. As scholar and activist, Vandana Shiva, writes, '[t]he colonies have now been extended to the interior spaces, the "genetic codes" of life-forms from microbes and plants to animals, including humans'.[1] Shiva terms the expropriation of Indigenous biological resources 'biopiracy', while other activists and critics apply the broader term 'biocolonialism' to the range of practices that extend colonialist logic to the acquisition of human and plant organic materials, genetic 'data', and medicinal knowledge. This term in particular highlights the marked continuities between European colonialist practices of land and resource appropriation and the research practices within what Laurelyn Whitt calls the 'new imperial science', which, 'marked by the confluence of science with capitalism' and acting 'in the service of western pharmaceutical ... industries' (among others), 'enabl[es] the appropriation of indigenous knowledge and resources at a prodigious and escalating rate'.[2]

The logic of biocolonial extractivism operates through a reorientation of the temporal formations of settler colonialism, which equate settler practices with development and consign Indigenous peoples to the past. The land dispossessions of the colonial era were facilitated by powerful narratives of inevitable Indigenous extinction: 'vanishing Indians', Māori and Aboriginal 'dying races'. As critics have shown, contemporary biocolonialist initiatives operate on similar assumptions, under which indigenous biospecimens must be preserved and biological data acquired before they vanish forever. Joanna Radin demonstrates that, since the mid-twentieth century, the ability to freeze and store blood and other organic samples has 'emerged as a potentially powerful strategy for preserving fragments of a world that appeared to be increasingly in flux'. It enables 'biological material to be studied in the present and especially in the future', when (whether due to genetic admixture, European diseases, or environmental damage produced by the industrialized global North) 'the individuals from whom it had been extracted were expected to have disappeared or changed beyond recognition'.[3]

In this article, I explore the intertwined relationship between medical research ethics and the logic and ideology of biocolonialism as it is represented in two contemporary American novels, Ann Patchett's *State of Wonder* (2011) and Hanya Yanagihara's *The People in the Trees* (2013). These novels depict 'medical adventurer[s]'[4] undertaking biocolonialist excursions into the remote jungles of, respectively, the Amazon and the Pacific, and are centrally concerned with the methods and infrastructure of biomedical and pharmaceutical research. In both cases, the fictional scientists' ethically problematic research practices implicate them in what Pauline Wakeford calls 'two entangled narratives of death and disappearance: the *grand récits* of wildlife extinction and the vanishing Indian'.[5] I focus in particular on how these texts, by presenting us with fictional bioethical quandaries related to human longevity and reproduction, engage with the new formulations of extinction discourse produced by the life sciences. Patrick Brantlinger asserts that colonial 'extinction discourse was performative in the sense that it acted on the world as well as described it'.[6] *State of Wonder* and *The People in the Trees* both imagine biological discoveries with the potential to extend human lifecycles, but these research endeavours are steeped in extinctionist ideology and themselves set in motion the decimation of previously thriving Indigenous communities. Aspirational narratives of 'eternal life' (in Yanagihara) and 'world health' (in Patchett) are underpinned by the knowledge that these communities, reframed as research subjects, are likely to vanish in the wake of what Warwick Anderson calls 'scientific colonialism', along with their unique ecosystems.[7] The different narrative temporalities of these texts – Patchett's anticipating a significant breakthrough in global health, Yanagihara's narrated retrospectively from a position of irreversible loss – produce divergent valuations of human and nonhuman lives and different perspectives on the ethics of biopiracy, as I shall discuss. But in reading them together, I demonstrate how fictional engagements with biocolonial science illuminate the continuities between colonial-era extractivism and contemporary research practices.

In their temporal reorientations and their ability to imagine actual and potential acts of extinction, these texts resituate extinction discourse squarely within the context of twentieth- and twenty-first-century bioscientific experimentation.

State of Wonder follows Marina Singh, a pharmacologist for a multinational pharmaceutical corporation, Vogel, on her expedition into the Amazon to investigate the death in the field of her colleague, Anders Eckman, and to assess the progress of a senior scientist, Annick Swenson, who is developing a fertility drug for Vogel while living with a remote tribe, the Lakashi. Swenson has discovered that the Lakashi women's practice of chewing bark from a particular local tree not only alters their reproductive chemistry, allowing them to conceive and give birth into their seventies and eighties, but also inoculates them against malaria. Alongside their work on the fertility drug, Swenson and her team are surreptitiously developing a malaria vaccine at Vogel's expense, which will have little appeal to company shareholders even though it 'will have enormous benefits to world health', since '[t]he people who need a malarial vaccine will never have the means to pay for it'.[8] As the narrative unfolds, the protection of the Lakashi, their lifeways, and their environment is pitted against this urgent global health imperative to save the lives of the '[e]ight hundred thousand children' who, as Swenson tells Marina, 'die every year of malaria' in the so-called 'Third World'.[9]

The People in the Trees is framed as the memoirs of Norton Perina, a 'renowned immunologist' who, as a young doctor in 1950, joins an anthropological expedition to U'ivu, a fictional Micronesian state.[10] Along with his anthropologist colleagues, he 'discovers' a 'lost tribe' living on the island of Ivu'ivu whose ritual ingestion of a sacred turtle endemic to the island, the opa'ivu'eke, causes extended longevity, with some tribe members apparently living for several hundred years. Perina's research on this phenomenon earns him a Nobel Prize for Medicine, but also kickstarts a rapid process of biocolonial incursion on this island that has 'never [before] been colonized', beginning with pharmaceutical companies, seeking to develop 'age-retarding drugs, ... anti-aging skin creams, [and] elixirs to restore male potency', all 'swarming throughout Ivu'ivu on the hunt for the opa'ivu'eke'.[11] It results in the extinction of the turtle, the razing of the island, and the decimation of the Ivu'ivuan community through an accelerated experience of the impacts of colonization, including forced displacement, alcoholism, and disease.

Both texts emphasize the overdetermination of their respective jungle environments by longstanding colonialist tropes of exotic difference that are inflected by bioscientific discourse. The Pacific island, as Elizabeth DeLoughrey has demonstrated, has long been figured as a remote, 'hermetically sealed laboratory', 'deemed ahistorical and isolated' from modernity and therefore ideal for experimentation in anthropology, ecology, and nuclear science.[12] The Amazon, meanwhile, is imagined as what Veronica Davidov terms a 'pharmacopia' that holds within its rich ecosystems 'fantastic cures for illnesses that defy the capacities of the Western pharmaceutical industry', or, as Dr Swenson puts it in *State of Wonder*, 'some sort of magical medicine chest'.[13] Under the globalized conditions of the biomedical and pharmaceutical industries, the jungle spaces outside the West are vulnerable to exploitation due to their construction as 'global commons' or 'global resource frontier[s]' available to be harvested for their medical riches.[14] As Swenson asserts in an unapologetic utilization of extractivist rhetoric: 'there is much to be taken from the jungle'.[15] Through their focus on the activities of life scientists in the interconnected fields of big pharma and global health, both novels appear to offer a critique of the impacts of biocolonialism on Indigenous people and the ecosystems in which they exist. But, as I will show, Perina's retrospective narration in *The People in the Trees* brings into critical focus the extinctionist logic of biocolonial science, while *State of Wonder's* anticipatory positioning is ultimately bound up with the future-oriented rhetoric used to justify much exploitative and damaging scientific research.

The People in the Trees introduces its Ivu'ivuan 'lost tribe' through the lens of 1950s anthropology. As an ambitious junior doctor on an anthropological expedition, Perina observes his anthropologist colleagues with a degree of scorn regarding their research activities, which seem to consist of conducting 'fruitless interviews with the dreamers' – the elderly Ivu'ivuans who have ingested opa'ivu'eke flesh and who are consequently aged between one and three hundred years old – and of 'filling entire notebooks with minute descriptions of the most mundane of activities'.[16] The text enacts a forensic examination of anthropological method and ideology, presenting us with anthropologists who are, in line with recent critiques of the discipline, 'entrenched in island boundedness, isolation, and atemporality' in this period before the field's critical turn.[17] In thematizing this mid-twentieth-century anthropological perspective on the Indigenous tribe, Yanagihara draws attention to anthropology's foundational role in establishing problematic research engagements with Indigenous people. The 'funereal but very modern science of anthropology', as Brantlinger terms it, was heavily implicated in, and dependent upon, extinction discourse 'in its attempt to learn as much as possible about primitive societies and cultures before they vanish forever'.[18]

The People in the Trees dramatizes what Johannes Fabian famously termed 'the denial of coevalness' – the assumption that supposedly 'primitive' Indigenous subjects of anthropological study exist on a different temporal plane from the 'modern' scientists studying them.[19] Yanagihara employs contrasting notions of time in Perina's account of the villagers and the scientists. The researchers obey a 'definition of time … determined in the part of the world where people consulted clocks and made and kept appointments' (consonant with Mark Rifkin's notion of 'settler time'), while in the Ivu'ivuan jungle, Perina recounts, 'time twirled itself into long, spiraling whorls, defying biology and evolution; not even the human body respected it'.[20] He understands the villagers to possess 'no notion of time, no notion of history', despite being aware of their 400-day year and system for measuring birthdays.[21] While extinction discourse in the colonial era was mobilized to make way for the settler, conveniently bypassing Indigenous sovereignty on the land with the assumption of their inevitable elimination, in this context of 1950s Pacific anthropology, the denial of coevalness makes way for biocolonial exploitation of natural resources and Indigenous knowledge. The research of the lead anthropologist, Paul Tallent, on a U'ivuan origin story linking the opa'ivu'eke to immortality, as well as on recent island histories rich in ecological and climatic knowledge, forms the basis for Perina's biomedical experimentation on the dreamers and turtles.

However, while anthropology as a discipline is certainly not exonerated regarding its complicity with biocolonial formations, Yanagihara's characterization of Tallent and Perina underlines the significant contrast in their ethical decision-making. Tallent is 'of Sioux extraction' and 'know[s] what it's like to be studied', having been subjected to intrusive physical examination in his orphanage at the hands of a phrenologist who is convinced that skull measurements prove that 'the Indians had been biologically ordained to lose their lands to the Europeans'.[22] This kind of racial pseudoscience, of course, underpinned nineteenth- and early twentieth-century extinction discourse, so Tallent's childhood experience of pathologization foreshadows the consequences of his own research with the Ivu'ivuans. Aware of the potential for the island's exploitation if the connection between longevity and ingesting turtle meat is publicized, Tallent protects this revelation, restricting his publications on the 'lost tribe' to knowledge that is '[c]ertainly of no profit to anyone'.[23]

Perina has no such qualms, and is introduced to the reader in a context of ethical turmoil. As a series of framing devices – two press releases and a preface to his memoirs – inform us, his life writing is undertaken in the late 1990s from prison, where he is serving a custodial sentence for the rape and sexual assault of one of the forty-three children he has adopted from U'ivu.[24] Deliberately and incongruously, Yanagihara juxtaposes Perina's intimate narrative voice with meticulous academic footnotes provided by his friend and self-appointed editor, Ronald Kubodera, M.D. These contexualize Perina's personal moral decision-making within the wider systemic structures in which biomedical science operates, serving not to confirm Perina's status as a 'great mind' as the acolyte editor intends, but rather to emphasize his institutional privilege.[25] While Perina self-presents as a maverick scientist, an iconoclastic institutional outsider whose rule-breaking is fundamental to scientific progress, his extraction of biomedical data, fauna, and knowledge from Ivu'ivu results, as Kubodera documents, in career-building publications, research funding, and professional prestige.

Perina's abuse of his children is intimately tied up with his dehumanizing professional treatment of their fellow U'ivuans. A physician with – beyond 'the unslakability of [his] intellectual thirst' – self-professedly 'no interest' in 'cur[ing] diseases', 'eradicat[ing] illnesses' or 'prolong[ing] life', Perina sees the 'dreamers' as less-than-human lab fodder – 'boring specimens to work with', 'not dissimilar to those dim white mice I had spent all those mornings killing' in the laboratory.[26] His medical tests are invasive and non-consensual, and he removes four of the dreamers from their island home, without their understanding or consent, and transports them to the United States heavily sedated. In 1950, he notes, this was 'back when you could do such things without ethics boards howling at you'.[27] Confined in Perina's US lab over subsequent decades, the dreamers are 'pricked and poked and swabbed and made to urinate in plastic cups (something they had never seen before)', and have 'substantial quantities of blood ... siphoned from their veins each week'.[28] Perina frames their resulting deterioration in energy and mental health in terms that tellingly echo dying race discourse: 'It was necessary, this work, and their decline was inevitable, but I still sentimentally wished it could have gone better for them.'[29]

Yanagihara carefully situates her narration of Perina's abuses within a wider history of racialized medical ethics. The dreamers are removed from Perina's care in 1975, 'after Willowbrook, after Tuskegee, after the birth of the National Commission for the Protection of Human Subjects of

Biomedical and Behavioral Research'.[30] Kubodera's three-page-long footnote documenting Perina's encounters with ethical review boards and the inadequacy of the dreamers' treatment after this removal, when they are ensconced in an American retirement community, offers a critical perspective on the efficacy of the ethics system in its early days. However, Yanagihara's detailed contextualization of the infrastructure of biomedical research leaves no doubt regarding Perina's individual culpability for both the direct mistreatment of research subjects and the scaled up, systemic biopiracy that follows his expeditions to Ivu'ivu. The narrative makes clear that the dreamers' initial removal from the island, along with a sacred opa'ivu'eke that Perina butchers and smuggles back to the USA for lab testing, constitute the island's founding acts of biopiracy.

The anti-biocolonial narrative in *The People in the Trees* is powerful because the lure of eternal life remains elusive, since Perina and his successors are unable to overcome the problem that the dreamers' condition can prevent physical ageing but not an age-related decline in mental faculties, and is pointedly disconnected from any narrative of global health benefit. *State of Wonder* seems to offer a similar critique when its focus is on Swenson's Vogel-funded fertility drug, which is represented in relatively clear-cut terms as a case of Indigenous TEK (the practice of bark chewing and its prevention of ova deterioration) being exploited to benefit wealthy global pharmaceutical consumers. Taking a self-righteous stance on reproductive agency by framing childbearing as a lifestyle choice, Swenson opines, 'I've never believed the women of the world are entitled to leave every one of their options open for a lifetime.'[31] After experimenting on herself and going through a pregnancy and dangerous stillbirth at the age of seventy-three, she moralizes towards the end of the novel that she has 'been punished' for 'straying into the territory of the biologically young' and revokes her plan to eventually deliver the drug she has spent years developing: 'Let the fifty-year-olds console themselves with in vitro as they have in the past.'[32] The manipulation of natural reproductive rhythms – the 'biological clock' – to meet consumer desires is presented as a luxury rather than a necessity, and one that could come at a huge cost to the delicately balanced ecosystem in which the Lakashi live.

But while the fertility plotline seems to open the way for anti-biocolonial critique, this is undermined by the revelation of the Lakashi women's resistance to malaria, which introduces a narrative of seemingly greater, and global, need. The fertility drug and the malaria vaccine are chemically 'intertwined', their effects both produced by a particular species of moths (purple martinets) laying eggs in the bark of a particular tree (the Martin tree), meaning that '[w]hen we get one drug we'll have the other'.[33] Swenson's exploitation of Indigenous ethnomedicinal resources is ultimately represented as justifiable in light of a 'fantasy of the common good'[34] – the appeal to the 'world health' benefits of a malaria vaccine – especially since her commitment to, as she puts it, making 'an American pharmaceutical company ... foot the bill for Third World do-gooding' seems subversive.[35] But while some postcolonial writers, as Jessica Howell argues, 'rewr[i]te the significance of malaria science and malarial illness ... in order to critique colonial and postcolonial health politics',[36] in the pharmaceutical imaginary of Patchett's text malaria is thematized only in terms of its inconvenience to first-world travellers, as for example when Marina experiences an extreme adverse reaction to the antimalarial drug, Lariam, as she prepares for her Vogel-funded expedition down the Rio Negro. 'World health', in contrast, operates as a somewhat empty signifier in this novel. It is exploited as a plot device that, as Shital Pravinchandra argues, 'effectively allow[s] Patchett to carefully re-write biocolonialism as a benevolent concern for the optimized health and longevity of the entire human species', even while it is used to justify the characters' flagrant breaches of medical ethics and present the potential extinction of the Lakashi as a fair price to pay for the solution to a global health crisis.[37]

In *State of Wonder*, set in the millennial period when ethical review boards *are* firmly established, medical surveillance of indigenous bodies has been naturalized: Swenson has transformed the Lakashi into 'patient subjects, submitting themselves to constant weighing and measurement, allowing their menstrual cycles to be charted and their children to be pricked for blood samples' in the service of the intertwined fertility and malarial research.[38] The Lakashi women routinely '[s]elf-swab' their vaginal fluid in order for the doctors to monitor 'the levels of estrogen in [their] cervical mucus',[39] while the men are regularly infected with malaria (without their informed consent) in order to act as a control group for the women, who are inoculated by the Martin bark. Swenson's stories of 'the tireless cajoling and gift giving that had once been required for even the most basic examinations' and her imperious declaration, 'I tamed them', leaves the reader in no doubt that the production of docile, compliant Lakashi research subjects is achieved through the medical colonization of their bodies and lifeways.[40]

As in *The People in the Trees*, Tuskegee features as an ethical touchstone in Patchett's text. 'Don't make this out to be the Tuskegee Institute',

Swenson's colleague, Alan Saturn, cautions Marina. 'The difference is that when they get it [malaria] in this room we're also going to cure it.'[41] The novel rather blithely acknowledges this landmark case in medical ethics in order to dismiss any comparison and to confirm, in contrast, the overarching benevolence of its scientists' actions. Saturn argues that 'It's good to get out of the American medical system from time to time', pitting the ethical stop-checks of this system – and the welfare of the infected men – against the global health benefits of the malaria vaccine: 'If they get sick for a couple of days in the name of developing a drug that could protect the entire tribe, the entire world, then I say so be it.'[42] In this self-exemption from ethical protocols, Saturn prioritizes global and heroic medical goals over the wellbeing of Indigenous patients and displays a deeply biocolonialist mindset regarding the relative worth of human lives. But while Marina feels 'a little uncomfortable with [Saturn's] argument', within the logic of the novel the moral certainty of the maverick scientists legitimately overrides the system of ethical review that is a basic requirement of field research in the life sciences.[43]

The consistently dehumanizing treatment of the Lakashi research subjects is premised on the fact that, like Perina, Swenson buys into the denial of coevalness, characterizing the Lakashi as 'an intractable race', impervious to '[a]ny progress you advance to them'.[44] Like the Ivu'ivuans, the Lakashi 'have no apparent system for marking time' as far as Swenson and her researchers (none of whom speak the Indigenous language) can tell, and the women's regularity in visiting a forest glade to chew the Martin bark is laughingly put down to the 'Lakashi biological clock', a designation that upholds stereotypes of Indigenous knowledge as instinctive and embodied rather than rational.[45] Their medicinal knowledge, too, is dismissed by Swenson as guesswork and superstition:

'I have very little respect for what passes as science around here. ... [f]or these people there is no concept of a dosage, no set lengths for treatments. When something works it seems to me to be nothing short of a miracle.'[46]

This declaration follows exactly the logic of biopiracy, according to which the colonialist practice of 'appropriat[ing] biodiversity from the original owners and innovators' is justified by 'defining their seeds, medicinal plants, and medical knowledge as nature, as nonscience'.[47] Swenson's construction of the Lakashi as intractable and their TEK as 'nonscience', then, is crucial to the proposed pharmaceutical exploitation of their ecosystem. For a malaria vaccine to be mass-produced and marketed, any Lakashi claim to the TEK must be undermined, an ideological move achieved by annexing them outside of scientific progress.

The novel's continuities with the extinctionist logic of high colonialism are most apparent in Swenson's declaration that

> 'You can't draw the world a map to this place and have everyone come running in, trampling the Rapps [a rare species of hallucinogenic mushroom], killing off the martinets, displacing the tribe. By the time they understood what they were doing, it would all be dead.'[48]

Here, the novel employs a distinctive rhetorical feature of extinction discourse, a construction that Brantlinger terms 'the future-perfect mode of proleptic elegy', which 'mourns the lost object before it is completely lost'.[49] This proleptic mode, which looks back at a future action from a projected point beyond its completion, functions to position Swenson as a protector of the tribe, someone who is buying the Lakashi time even while confirming the inevitability of their demise (which is, of course, in her hands, since she does eventually intend to publicize at least the malaria research). Moreover, she reframes her extractive fertility research as, ironically, the gift of time freely given by the Lakashi to the world at large: 'There will be nothing but time, don't you understand? That's what the Lakashi are offering.'[50] The disingenuousness here resembles what Wakeford identifies as a 'semiotics of taxidermy' in various contemporary spheres of Indigenous encounter including ethnographic representations and genomic research. As a mode of representation that suggests 'the conquest of time and mortality through the preservation of the semblance of life in death', in taxidermic figurations 'the denial of coevalness is reinvented and reinscribed through various forms of time-lagging and time-warping', temporal manipulations that once more relegate Indigenous subjects to the past and 'find fresh ways to reinforce fantasies of colonial mastery in the current era'.[51] In Swenson's ruminations, biocolonial mastery is secured by rendering the Lakashi as taxidermic specimens of biomedical research: their own survival is impossible but their legacy is preserved through the gift of time (via the fertility drug), and of life itself (via the malaria vaccine), that they will offer to the world.

In the most material terms, the Lakashi are subject to taxidermic time-warping through their frozen biosamples, indefinitely preserved, that will result in the production of these medicines. As Radin explains, biocolonial ideology is characterized by the investment of the life sciences in the 'as yet unknown' uses of frozen biospecimens.[52] Facilitating the preservation of human tissue in a state somewhere between life and death, the freezer functions 'as a time capsule, a means of making a biological freeze-frame for the future'.[53] In *State of Wonder*, in the heart of the jungle, 'the blood samples in the freezers [are] flash-frozen to arctic levels', their value immeasurable.[54] Towards the end of the novel, after the stillbirth delivery of Swenson's child, born with a condition, '*Sirenomelia, Mermaid Syndrome*', characterized by fused legs and no visible genitalia, 'the freezer where they stored the blood samples' also becomes 'the same freezer where she kept the child with the curving tail' in anticipation of testing the baby's body 'to see what levels of the compound are in the tissues'.[55] The father of this child is never disclosed by Swenson, but is likely Lakashi, and the placement of the infant in the freezer alongside Lakashi blood samples functions as a symbol, in the text's logic, of inevitable and rightful demise. Born to a seventy-three-year-old white woman, this seemingly unnatural child cannot be allowed to survive without irreparably altering the Western world's expectations of women's 'biological clocks'. But for the Lakashi, in Swenson's opinion, bearing 'late-life children' is their 'particular fate', and one that confirms their exclusion from modernity and their unfitness for survival in the contemporary world.[56] The Lakashi must die out or be displaced from their habitat in order for the Martins and martinets to be harvested, and with this destruction of their ecosystem will come the end of their extended fertility. The frozen infant, itself with no discernible physiological means of reproduction, serves as a proleptic relic of Lakashi reproductive difference, preserving the biochemical traces of the Martins' impact on fertility even while it anticipates the inevitable – and 'natural' – erasure of their practice of late-life pregnancy.

In *The People in the Trees*, there is no such sense that the demise of the Ivu'ivuans – or the opa'ivu'ekes – is an inevitable restoration of natural order. The consequences of Perina's abuses are narrated, from the 1990s, in an extraordinary passage spanning several pages that Eleanor Byrne describes as a 'confession of ecocide' and an 'archive of extinction'.[57] Here, Perina performs temporal reorientations by accelerating the telling of these events at the heart of the narrative. He prefaces his catalogue of devastation with the statement that 'You know, we all know, what happened next',[58] but combined with the intimate rhetorical formulation, 'shall I tell you?', this positions the reader simultaneously in the narrative present, armed with hindsight regarding the technoscientific violence wrought on the island, and in the process of this violence unfolding:

Shall I tell you of how the pharmacists and neuroscientists and biologists hurried home with their carrier bags heavy with turtles[?] ... Shall I tell you of how by the time telomeres were discovered, and then by the time genetic sequencing became sophisticated enough to conjecture exactly how the opa'ivu'eke was affecting normal telomerase, there were no more opa'ivu'ekes to be studied? ... shall I tell you how the island was stripped of everything, whole forests razed[?][59]

The accelerated narration of these incursions mirrors the accelerated experience of colonization that pharmaceutical extractivism brings to U'ivu. In the space of a decade – a decade characterized by *de*colonization elsewhere in the world – the small but stable island community is forced through all the stages of colonization and cultural fragmentation that Indigenous populations worldwide experienced during decades and centuries of European colonialism: land dispossession and ecological depletion; conversions to Western religions; exposure to alcohol and venereal diseases; industrialization and new labour practices; dietary transformations, and so on.[60] As Perina writes, 'there are really no new stories in cases like these'.[61] The 'newness' here is in the scientific impetus behind *bio*colonial fatal impact   the major players in the island's destruction being pharmaceutical corporations along with US and European universities – and the speed with which it precipitates the extinction of the opa'ivu'eke and the transformation beyond recognition (or the disappearance, if we buy into anthropological notions of Indigenous cultures as static, bounded, and pure) of Ivu'ivuan lifeways.

The central irony of this text lies in the 'time-warping' fact that the incursion of the biopirates results in the extinction of the life-extending turtle species before the biological mechanism causing this effect – the inactivation of telomerase – can be fully identified or replicated. There is no contemplation of 'as yet unknown' bioscientific knowledge emerging from the time capsule of the freezer in this text; Perina's account 'of Pfizer's sorrow, of Lilly's dismay, of Johnson and Johnson's agony, of Merck's rage' makes it clear that the promise of eternal life has died with the opa'ivu'eke.[62] Unlike Patchett, then, Yanagihara does not buy into either the proleptic assumption of inevitable disappearance or the compensatory narrative of preserved 'biovalue' built into what Radin terms 'salvage biology'.[63] Instead, she presents the opa'ivu'ekes' extinction as a fait accompli, an irreversible loss that is produced entirely by human activity and is thus entirely preventable. She tells what Deborah Bird Rose, Thom van Dooren and Matthew Chrulew call an 'extinction story', a genealogy of a species' decline that 'grapple[s] with, and respond[s] to, the complexity and ethical significance of specific sites of loss'.[64]

But while the turtles are gone forever in this narrative, the dreamers are purportedly preserved in a state of death-in-life, reduced to biospecimens, their bodies transformed into biomedical cyborgs:

[T]here were stories that [the remaining dreamers on Ivu'ivu] were divvied up like candies by the pharmaceutical companies and flown away to live their lives in sterile labs, where they may be living still, punctured with needles, their arms sprouting tangles of IVs, their legs harvested for scrapings of skin, of muscle, of bone[.][65]

In this nightmarish scenario, these Indigenous elders, affected by a condition that preserves youth, are physically *unable* to conveniently die out in the way that extinction discourse demands in order to justify their exploitation. The only 'vanishing Indian' in this novel, in fact, turns out to be Tallent, whose mysterious disappearance into the jungle of Ivu'ivu at the height of the island's pillaging is interpreted by his biographer as 'self-inflicted penance' for his role in its exploitation.[66] This dual rewriting of the colonialist trope therefore resists any narrative of 'natural' Indigenous decline and retains a firm sense of the researchers' culpability. The still-living dreamers haunt the narrative present in a material, embodied form that disallows the erasure of Indigenous presence or their relegation to the past.

The People in the Trees, then, presents us with a much more *critical* rendering of biopiracy's 'new' extinction discourse than does *State of Wonder*. Patchett's text is future-oriented, leaving us in anticipation of the decimation of the Lakashi and the despoliation of their environment through the invasions yet to come, but 'compensating' for this with the knowledge that their loss will be for the sake of the malaria-stricken global poor. The devastation wrought by biopiracy remains conditional in this narrative, part of a not-yet-arrived future, and in light of the novel's thematic investment in future science (the hope of a malaria vaccine) this anticipatory mode renders the text complicit with biocolonialism's 'new', scientifically oriented, extinction discourse. By approaching wildlife extinction retrospectively while simultaneously making it impossible for its indigenous tribe to die out, Yanagihara's text resists any such reinscription of the ideology of extinction discourse. *The People in the Trees*, spanning the late twentieth century, critically historicizes the emergence of recognizably biocolonial research formations and situates its narrative in relation to the reactive – and woefully belated – development of medical ethics. The retrospective narration in this novel looks back upon the process of cultural and ecological degradation from a point of irreversible damage to the people and ecosystem of Ivu'ivu and gives us no sense that this cost has been worth paying. Rather than anticipating extinction, this novel shows instead how medical research ethics can and should be built upon the anticipation, and interrogation, of future applications of biomedical discovery.

ACKNOWLEDGEMENTS
Research for this article was funded by a Wellcome Trust Seed Award. I am grateful to Hamilton Carroll and Shirley Chew for their insightful feedback, and to Shital Pravinchandra for lively conversations about these texts.

NOTES

1. Vandana Shiva, *Biopiracy: The Plunder of Nature and Knowledge* (Cambridge, MA: South End Press, 1997), p. 3.
2. Laurelyn Whitt, *Science, Colonialism, and Indigenous Peoples: The Cultural Politics of Law and Knowledge* (Cambridge: Cambridge UP, 2009), p. xiv. See also the website and publications of the Indigenous Peoples' Council on Biocolonialism: <www.ipcb.org> accessed 26 March 2019.
3. Joanna Radin, *Life on Ice: A History of New Uses for Cold Blood* (Chicago and London: U of Chicago P, 2017), p. 56. Indigenous activist groups such as the Indigenous Peoples' Council on Biocolonialism have adeptly deconstructed the extinctionist logic tied up with numerous contemporary research initiatives, particularly the Human Genome Diversity Project. See, for example, Jenny Reardon, *Race to the Finish: Identity and Governance in an Age of Genomics* (Princeton, NJ: Princeton UP, 2005).
4. Hanya Yanagihara, *The People in the Trees* ([2013]; London: Picador, 2018), p. 33.
5. Pauline Wakeford, *Taxidermic Signs: Reconstructing Aboriginality* (Minneapolis: U of Minnesota P, 2008), p. 18.
6. Patrick Brantlinger, *Dark Vanishings: Discourse on the Extinction of Primitive Races, 1800-1930* (Ithaca and London: Cornell UP, 2003), p. 4.
7. Warwick Anderson, *The Collectors of Lost Souls: Turning Kuru Scientists into Whitemen* (Baltimore: The Johns Hopkins UP, 2008), p. 134.
8. Ann Patchett, *State of Wonder* (London: Bloomsbury, 2012), p. 319.
9. Patchett, *State of Wonder*, p. 319.
10. Yanagihara, *The People in the Trees*, p. 3.
11. Yanagihara, *The People in the Trees*, pp. 69, 250, 284.
12. Elizabeth M. DeLoughrey, *Routes and Roots: Navigating Caribbean and Pacific Island Literatures* (Honolulu: U of Hawai'i P, 2007), pp. 2, 16.
13. Veronica Davidov, 'Amazon as Pharmacopia', *Critique of Anthropology*, 33:3 (2013) 243-62, p. 249; Patchett, *State of Wonder*, p. 180.
14. Davidov, 'Amazon as Pharmacopia', pp. 244, 248.
15. Patchett, *State of Wonder*, p. 180.
16. Yanagihara, *The People in the Trees*, p. 160.
17. DeLoughrey, *Routes and Roots*, p. 16.
18. Brantlinger, *Dark Vanishings*, p. 5.
19. Johannes Fabian, *Time and the Other: How Anthropology Makes Its Object* (New York: Columbia UP, 1983).
20. Yanagihara, *The People in the Trees*, p. 213; Mark Rifkin, *Beyond Settler Time: Temporal Sovereignty and Indigenous Self-Determinism* (Durham and London: Duke UP, 2017).
21. Yanagihara, *The People in the Trees*, pp. 119, 141.
22. Yanagihara, *The People in the Trees*, pp. 75, 88.
23. Yanagihara, *The People in the Trees*, p. 246.
24. The novel is loosely based on the story of Carleton Gajdusek (1923-2008), a researcher for the US National Institutes of Health, with whom Yanagihara's oncologist father worked at NIH. Gajdusek's research in the 1950s and 60s on kuru, a fatal brain disease affecting the Fore people of Papua New Guinea, won him a 1976

Nobel Prize. He adopted many Melanesian and Micronesian children, and in 1997 served a 12-month prison sentence after pleading guilty to child molestation. Gajdusek's work (like Perina's) was carried out 'just before the widespread acceptance of ethics protocols and institutional review boards'. Anderson, *The Collectors of Lost Souls*, p. 6. See Anderson for a nuanced account of the ethical complexity of kuru research, particularly regarding Gajdusek's procurement of Fore brains for dissemination to research institutions in the global North.

25. Yanagihara, *The People in the Trees*, p. 9. Kubodera's own ethical qualms about Perina's actions, stubbornly repressed for most of the novel, surface in his excision and then reinstatement in a postscript of a passage in which Perina describes raping his adopted son Vincent (pp. 357-62).

26. Yanagihara, *The People in the Trees*, pp. 87, 108, 172.

27. Yanagihara, *The People in the Trees*, p. 229.

28. Yanagihara, *The People in the Trees*, p. 231.

29. Yanagihara, *The People in the Trees*, p. 275.

30. Yanagihara, *The People in the Trees*, p. 285. Willowbrook was a 1963-66 research study in which institutionalized intellectually disabled children were deliberately infected with hepatitis A in order to study that disease. Tuskegee refers to the infamous syphilis study (1932-72) carried out by the US Public Health Service, wherein African-American syphilitic men were monitored but left untreated, despite widespread and effective use of penicillin. The resulting scandal prompted developments in legal protections for clinical research participants and contributed to the establishment of informed consent as a requirement of biomedical research.

31. Patchett, *State of Wonder*, p. 317.

32. Patchett, *State of Wonder*, pp. 274, 344.

33. Patchett, *State of Wonder*, pp. 318, 319.

34. Davidov, 'Amazon as Pharmacopia', p. 249.

35. Patchett, *State of Wonder*, p. 319.

36. Jessica Howell, *Malaria and Victorian Fictions of Empire* (Cambridge: Cambridge UP, 2019), pp. 20-1.

37. Shital Pravinchandra, *Same Difference: Postcolonial Studies in the Age of Life Science* (unpublished manuscript).

38. Patchett, *State of Wonder*, p. 235.

39. Patchett, *State of Wonder*, pp. 288, 289.

40. Patchett, *State of Wonder*, p. 235.

41. Patchett, *State of Wonder*, p. 325.

42. Patchett, *State of Wonder*, p. 325.

43. Patchett, *State of Wonder*, p. 325.

44. Patchett, *State of Wonder*, p. 179.

45. Patchett, *State of Wonder*, pp. 281, 289. Just as the opa'ivu'eke are unique to Ivu'ivu in Yanagihara's fictional world, the ecological stakes are similarly high in Patchett's: the ecosystem consisting of the purple martinet moths, Martin trees, and Rapp mushrooms is exclusive to the Lakashis' specific area of the rain forest.

46. Patchett, *State of Wonder*, pp. 180-1.

47. Shiva, *Biopiracy*, p. 4.

48. Patchett, *State of Wonder*, pp. 316-17.

49. Brantlinger, *Dark Vanishings*, p. 4.

50. Patchett, *State of Wonder*, p. 271.

51. Wakeford, *Taxidermic Signs*, pp. 6, 17.

52. Radin, *Life on Ice*, p. 4.

53. Radin, *Life on Ice*, p. 3.
54. Patchett, *State of Wonder*, p. 233.
55. Patchett, *State of Wonder*, p. 360 (original emphasis), p. 357.
56. Patchett, *State of Wonder*, p. 274.
57. Eleanor Byrne, 'Ecogothic Dislocations in Hanya Yanagihara's *The People in the Trees*', *Interventions*, 19:7 (2017) 962-75, p. 970.
58. Yanagihara, *The People in the Trees*, p. 282.
59. Yanagihara, *The People in the Trees*, pp. 282-4.
60. In interview, Yanagihara reveals that the colonization of U'ivu is modelled on that of Hawai'i, where she grew up. 'Episode 23 – Hanya Yanagihara: *The People in the Trees* – Part 2', *This Writing Life* podcast, 6 August 2015, <https://thiswritinglife.co.uk/e/episode-23-hanya-yanagihara-2014-part-2/#more-5755938>.
61. Yanagihara, *The People in the Trees*, p. 289.
62. Yanagihara, *The People in the Trees*, p. 284.
63. Radin, *Life on Ice*, p. 6. 'Biovalue' is Catherine Waldby's term; see 'Stem Cells, Tissue Cultures, and the Production of Biovalue', *Health: An Interdisciplinary Journal for the Social Study of Health, Illness and Medicine*, 6:3 (2002) 305-23.
64. Deborah Bird Rose, Thom van Dooren, and Matthew Chrulew, 'Introduction: Telling Extinction Stories', *Extinction Studies: Stories of Time, Death, and Generations*, eds, Deborah Bird Rose, Thom van Dooren, and Matthew Chrulew (New York: Columbia UP, 2017), pp. 1-17, p. 3.
65. Yanagihara, *The People in the Trees*, p. 285.
66. Yanagihara, *The People in the Trees*, p. 246.

Hippocrates the Fool: Faith and Healing in Lovelich's *History of the Holy Grail*

KATHERINE STORM HINDLEY

'[A]s a literary monument, or as a work of art, his *History of the Holy Grail* is valueless', wrote Dorothy Kempe, one of the early-twentieth-century editors of the works of Henry Lovelich.[1] Other critics describe Lovelich as 'the most clumsy and tedious poet of the fifteenth century', and as 'an unimaginative and insensitive clod'.[2] The *History of the Holy Grail*, meanwhile, has been dismissed as a mere translation into English of the French *Estoire del Saint Graal* 'without any additions or alterations whatsoever', evidence only of the fact that Lovelich 'felt unfulfilled by his trade as a furrier'.[3] It is only relatively recently that some scholars, including Roger Dalrymple and Raluca Radulescu, have started to identify elements of originality within his verse.[4] In this article, I aim to show that, far from slavishly following his French source, Lovelich made significant, systematic changes that profoundly alter the text's approach to ideas of faith and healing. To do this I focus on just one short section of the *History of the Holy Grail*: the chapter dealing with the life and shameful death of the great physician Hippocrates, widely known in medieval England as Ypocras.[5]

In medical texts, Hippocrates was highly revered. Works from the Hippocratic corpus were assigned in medical schools, as were commentaries explaining them in further detail.[6] In one manuscript, the British Library's Sloane MS 6, Hippocrates and Galen are depicted together as the only human physicians in a series of drawings showing the development of medicine through Apollo and Asclepius.[7] Presented last, Hippocrates and Galen appear as the pinnacle of medical advancement. However, respect from medical practitioners did not save Hippocrates from criticism in literary texts, in which he appears variously as an arsonist, a murderer, and – as here – a lovesick fool.[8] Lovelich's English poem takes several steps to lessen the impact of Ypocras's worst failings, both by omitting long passages from his source, the thirteenth-century French prose *Estoire del Saint Graal*, and by altering important details. Simultaneously, he sharpens the misogyny of the French source by emphasizing the faults of the female characters with whom Ypocras interacts.

Still more significantly, as I argue below, Lovelich's alterations introduce considerable ambiguity into the text's discussion of medicine and miracle. Although the text at no point challenges the idea that Christ performed miracles while Ypocras practised medicine, it does point to the problem of discerning the cause of a patient's recovery. The issue Lovelich's changes explore is not the boundary between miracle and medicine, but the difficulty of assigning an unexpected recovery to one category or the other. The narrative maintains a Christian vision of the world in which miracle cures are superior to medical ones, while simultaneously raising the question of how to know what exactly has occurred. This is in striking contrast to the French source, which never allows for confusion between earthly medicine and miraculous healing. In repeated alterations to his source, Lovelich removes details that would have allowed the reader to discern from the text – rather than from extra-textual understanding of Christ's power – what has caused each of the astonishing recoveries the chapter describes.

Lovelich's *History of the Holy Grail* survives in just one manuscript copy, Cambridge, Corpus Christi College, MS 80. Its opening pages are missing and the text is prefaced by a disparaging Latin addition to a flyleaf reading 'Oh, what great labours this author expended on implausible things.'[9] The poem itself traces the early history of the Holy Grail as it travels from the Holy Land to Great Britain, and, although part of the Arthurian cycle, is set well before the birth of King Arthur. The chapter dealing with Ypocras is set even further in the past: the story is told after three characters in the main narrative are shipwrecked on an island on which they discover Ypocras's tomb and long-ruined home. Although the historical physician lived from the fifth to the fourth century before Christ, the Ypocras of the poem lives during Christ's lifetime.

The basic story in both the French and English versions is the same. It begins when Ypocras arrives in Rome and saves the life of the Augustus Caesar's nephew, who was thought to have died. Two statues, one of Ypocras and one of his patient, are erected in celebration of the wondrous cure. A beautiful woman sees the statues and sets out to prove that Ypocras does not deserve such an honour, as he cannot really have raised the dead. She takes advantage of the fact that Ypocras has fallen in love with her to trick him and humiliate him. As a result, the emperor removes the statues. Some time later a knight comes to Rome, bringing news of Christ's miracles. Ypocras decides to travel to Galilee to see them for himself, but he is distracted at the port by the apparent death of the son of the king of Persia. He heals the son and remains with the king. Eventually he marries a princess who hates him.[10] After several attempts, his wife succeeds in poisoning him thanks to information he has incautiously given her about antidotes. He dies and is buried on the island where he lived, and where his tomb is later found by the characters in the main narrative of the text.

The *History of the Holy Grail* as a whole takes the view that no man can defend himself against a wicked woman's wiles. Just a few chapters before the story of Ypocras, for example, the reader is presented with the story of King Solomon, in which Lovelich asserts that when a woman puts her mind to deception, 'wit of non liveng Man verament / Schal hire withstonde of hire Concettying'.[11] Ypocras's last words, 'that man Is born In non londe / [...] / that Kan be war of wommenes wyle, / So ful they ben of qweyntise & Gyle', echo that sentiment.[12] In the English version of the text, women are implicitly criticized both for being deceivers and for being deceived. For example, while in the French text the emperor erects the celebratory statue of Ypocras, Lovelich attributes this to the empress.[13] Declaring that Ypocras has made her 'A glad wommman', she remarks that 'A Man from deth to lyve A en Arere, / Thus dyde Neuere feciscyan, I trowe, Ere'.[14] A woman is therefore the first to make the erroneous claim that Ypocras has raised the dead. Her subsequent actions spread this belief: she has two golden statues made as a sign of her gratitude, one of Ypocras and one of the man he saved, with an inscription stating that Ypocras is 'the worthiest Phelesophre þat Evere was'.[15] She commands that the statues never be removed. Unlike in the French, the inscription given by the English poem does not explicitly say that Ypocras brought the nephew from death to life, but that he 'Arerid In Certeine / A man to lyve Owt of gret peyne'.[16] As the word 'arerid' can mean either 'restored to health', 'resurrected', or 'saved', the specific claim made in the inscription is not necessarily inaccurate.[17] Nevertheless, the people of Rome overestimate Ypocras's skills, interpreting them as miracle rather than medicine. They 'Cleped hym half A god', and 'As Moche worschepe to his fygure gonnen they do / As to Ony of here goddis dyden they tho'.[18]

A woman also causes Ypocras to be shamed on account of these statues. A beautiful traveller from Galilee, she rejects the statues on the grounds that it is impossible to raise a man 'From deth to lyve', and declares that she will make a fool of Ypocras.[19] Although her trick is not directly related to the question of medicine and miracle, the implication is that by publicly shaming Ypocras, she will have provided evidence against the claim that he might have performed a resurrection. Ypocras knows that her intention is to make a fool of him, yet the first time he sees her he becomes so lovesick that he is brought to the point of death. Lovesickness was both a common feature of romance texts and considered to be a potentially fatal medical reality for which the patient was not at fault.[20] Exploiting his condition, the woman suggests a way for Ypocras to visit her privately in her rooms at the top of a tower: he should climb into the vessel used to bring food to the prince of Babylon, who is imprisoned there, and she will pull the vessel up to her window. At this point the English text makes the first of the three major omissions in the Ypocras narrative noted in Furnivall's nineteenth-century edition.[21]

In the French version of the text, the reader is explicitly told that the woman is lying about the vessel. The prince is not imprisoned in the tower, nor is the barrel used to carry food. Instead, it is known as the 'Vessel of Judgment', and is used to display condemned criminals to the citizens of Rome before their executions, as all the Roman citizens know.[22] In the French text, therefore, Ypocras is not fooled in part because he fails to recognize what is apparently an obvious lie about the city he has been living in. Lovelich's English translation, by contrast, gives its reader no reason to suppose that the woman's story about the prince is untrue until after Ypocras has climbed into the vessel and been pulled part-way up the tower. While the reader knows that she intends to trick Ypocras, it is unclear how the vessel fits into her plans.[23] It is only once Ypocras has left the ground but has not yet been fastened in the air that we learn that he is being drawn up by 'this lady and hire Owne Cosyn / be whom was wrowht this fals Engyn'.[24] The vessel itself has evidently been built for the exclusive purpose of tricking Ypocras, and the citizens of Rome merely suppose that it is being used for punishment.[25] The woman has therefore put greater effort into her trick, but has displayed less ingenuity than the woman in the French text who exploits her surroundings to her benefit.

The second major alteration to the text further reduces the emphasis on the intelligence of the lady from Galilee in outwitting Ypocras, and also removes a clear reminder that her trick is linked to her opinion that Ypocras cannot have raised the dead. It seems possible that the omission here is the result of an error in copying, since the text is ungrammatical, cutting off the emperor's speech in the middle of a sentence.[26] Nevertheless, the omission alters the effect of the passage. In the English version, the emperor sees Ypocras suspended in the vessel and orders him to be brought down. When Ypocras refuses to explain how he came to be there, the emperor immediately destroys the two statues. In the French text, when Ypocras refuses to explain himself the woman has a painting placed in front of the statues that shows him being pulled up in the vessel by two women. When the emperor orders it to be removed, the woman intervenes to argue that the painting shows a true event while the statues depict Ypocras restoring the dead to life, an impossible event that cannot have happened. This persuades Ypocras to her side, and he tells the emperor that if the statues are not removed he will leave Rome. The removal of the statues therefore hinges on the question of whether or not the event they depict is plausible.

In Lovelich's French source, the emphasis is on the woman's reasoning and strength of logic, as she forces Ypocras to view the statues in the way she wishes. The English preserves the sentence that, in the French, stresses this fact: 'it to-broken ne hadden they not ben / Ne hadde þe damyseles speche ben as I wen'.[27] In the English, however, the only speech to which that might refer is the mocking comment the woman makes when Ypocras is suspended in the vessel: 'let se what oure phelesophie Can don / Owther vpe to brynge, outher down Agayn; / e scholen it now preven In Certein'.[28] In the English there is therefore more focus on Ypocras's embarrassment at his situation, without the corresponding emphasis on the wit of the woman who outsmarted him or on the fact that she is right about what Ypocras's treatment actually accomplished.

Although Lovelich reduces the emphasis on the Galilean traveller's opinions about medicine and miracle, he also makes changes which raise questions about the status of medicine more generally. Specifically, he removes passages which clarify for the reader whether a specific instance of healing was achieved through miraculous or medical means. The section discussing Ypocras stands out within Lovelich's *History of the Holy Grail* as the only instance of earthly healing by a non-Christian physician. Aside from the cures performed by Ypocras, the text presents successful healing not as the result of earthly medical skill but as a product of divine intervention. Before Ypocras appears in the narrative the reader encounters several examples of explicitly Christian healing. Sarracynte's mother suffers from a wasting sickness that is healed through prayer, and receives baptism shortly afterwards. Although she has spent 'Certeinlye / More thane xv thowsend besaunz' on doctors, she only recovers her health through faith in Christ.[29] Evalach's shield, which is decorated with a cross on which the crowd see a vision of the crucified Christ, miraculously restores a man's severely wounded arm.[30] An angel heals a spear-wound in Joseph's hip and restores Nasciens' sight.[31] These stories align bodily with spiritual health. The same pattern continues after the Ypocras chapter. Wounds are healed by the sign of the cross, in allegorical stories of kissing roses that represent the Virgin Mary, and miraculously by the blood of the murdered King Lancelot.[32] Only one instance of earthly healing appears besides those performed by Ypocras, and even that takes on a religious aspect when a Christian doctor, repeatedly and insistently described in terms of his religion, uses medicinal herbs to treat wounds that non-Christian doctors have been unable to cure.[33]

Lovelich opens his story with the assertion that the non-Christian Ypocras was 'the worthiest Fecyscian that was / Evere Acompted In Ony plas; / For of that Scyense More Coude he / than ony Man leveng In Cristiente'.[34] This is already a significant promotion for Ypocras, who in the French *Graal* is only the foremost among 'all the men who were dominant in his time and who had worked long and diligently at this science'.[35] Where the French text implies that later physicians surpassed Ypocras's skill, Lovelich asserts that his preeminence extends into the audience's Christian present, complicating the pattern elsewhere in the text that associates successful healing with Christian faith. Lovelich also begins here to blur the distinction between medicine and miracle by adding that Ypocras's worth was described as 'Passenge Al Erthly men Many fold'.[36] Although the medieval audience would have known that Ypocras could not perform miracles, Lovelich's claim implies that his cures might nevertheless appear miraculous because of the extent to which his skill surpassed that of other earthly physicians. As soon as Ypocras is introduced in the English translation, therefore, the audience is primed to expect his feats of healing to go beyond what would be normal, and even to exceed what would be seen as natural.

The first cure Ypocras performs is the explicitly non-miraculous healing of Augustus Caesar's nephew, discussed above. This cure is not as marvellous as it appears to those who witness it. Ypocras, like the reader, hears of the emperor's nephew's death from 'A lytel Child' who reports that in Rome 'they seyn that ded Is he'.[37] However, when Ypocras examines the nephew we are told that 'lyf In his Body thanne felte he'.[38] Only when he realizes that the nephew is alive does he begin treatment. The reader is therefore immediately and explicitly aware that Ypocras knew his patient was alive, and that the empress is misled when she praises him for raising a man from death to life. Lovelich is also careful to remind the reader that Ypocras's success is due not only to his skill but also to the 'gret vertu' in the juice of the unspecified herb that he puts into his patient's mouth, in line with the common medieval claim that God's virtue is in words, stones, and herbs.[39]

While it is clear to the reader that Ypocras has not performed a miracle, it is equally clear that the people of Rome believe that a miracle has occurred. As the 'lytel Child' states, the emperor's nephew was thought to have died following a long illness. The people of Rome, including the empress, react to his recovery with astonishment. As mentioned above, they even begin to worship him as a god. In the French, this error of discernment between medicine and miracle is attributed only to 'the poor, who were quite ignorant'.[40] The learned instead praise Ypocras's wisdom, recognizing his knowledge and skill rather than imagining him to have supernatural abilities. In refusing to differentiate the responses of educated and uneducated audiences, the English text implies a greater difficulty in distinguishing between miraculous healing and the exceptionally skilled medicine practised by Ypocras. Textual evidence, such as the inscription on the statue discussed above, and physical evidence, such as the recovery of patients, are both presented as ambiguous.

In Lovelich's version, we are told that the people of Rome would have worshipped Ypocras 'for Evere More' were it not for the intervention of the traveller from Galilee who refuses to believe that anyone can raise a man 'From deth to lyve'.[41] Her ire is focused entirely on the physician, rather than on 'those who made these statues', as in the French.[42] Although it is clear that the woman from Galilee is correct that Ypocras has not raised anyone from the dead, her place of origin complicates her assertion that it is an impossible task. Once again, this is an alteration from the French version, in which she comes from Gaul. In having her come from Galilee, Lovelich places her in the very region in which Christ is miraculously performing the deeds she denies are possible. As the audience might have been aware, one of the miracles performed in Galilee even involves raising the dead daughter of Jairus, although unlike Christ's other such miracles this one is kept secret.[43]

Although Christ has not yet been mentioned directly within the Ypocras narrative, the story takes place 'Whanne Augustus Cesar Emperour was', locating it around the time of Christ's youth. This, combined with the reference to Galilee, means that the reader must think twice when the woman insists that raising the dead 'may not be trewe In non Manere; / Ne neuere beleven it In my thowht / For non Man that Evere was wrowht'.[44] Taking the technical meaning of the word 'wrowht', the woman from Galilee is referring to created men, a category that does not include the Son of God. In its more idiomatic meaning, however, her phrase refers to any living man, Christ included. In either interpretation the woman is ignorant of the power of the saints and Old Testament prophets to raise the dead, drawing on power delegated to them by God.[45] Her assertion is theologically correct in terms of earthly ability, but it ignores the abilities God gives to certain created men. Once again, Lovelich raises the question of how to distinguish medical cures from miraculous ones.

The question of discerning true miracles becomes more urgent with the appearance of a knight who arrives in Rome with stories of healing miracles performed by 'A pore Man'.[46] Nothing in the knight's account indicates that the man working these wonders is more than ordinarily human and, unlike in the French, the knight does not claim to have seen the miracles himself. As it would have been clear to the audience that the person described is Christ and that the miracles are true miracles, Ypocras's assertion that he can cure the same conditions emphasizes the same ambiguity that Lovelich hints at in his earlier alterations to the French source. Two linguistic echoes emphasize the comparison between Ypocras and Christ. First, Ypocras knows more about medicine 'than ony Man leveng', while the knight bringing news of Christ declares that he will tell Ypocras the most marvellous thing ever heard 'of Ony Man leveng'.[47] This parallel is not present in the French, which instead says that the story is the most marvellous ever heard 'about a man of that country'.[48] Second, when the knight insists that Christ can cure more diseases that Ypocras, he stresses that Christ's miracles are performed 'Openly In Mennys siht'.[49] This echoes the emperor's nephew rising fully healed 'Openly there In Alle Mennes Syht', a line that does not appear in the French.[50] In Lovelich's version, therefore, the text itself displays the similarity between the two cures in terms of what an external observer might witness, or hear from common rumour. The primary difference between the two is that Christ heals men 'by his wordis', while Ypocras uses herbal remedies.[51]

Ypocras's reaction to the knight's story reminds the reader that reports are unreliable. While he is impressed by the knight's claims, he does not immediately believe them. To the Christian readers of the poem it is clear that the knight is describing divine miracles, but to Ypocras, who has seen his own works exaggerated, the deeds the knight describes seem to be beyond 'alle Erthly Creature' – as indeed they are.[52] This language echoes the earlier description of Ypocras being judged as having skill beyond 'Al Erthly men Many fold', a connection which suggests a justification for Ypocras's doubt.[53] Ypocras tells the knight that he will travel to Galilee 'Forto Se / And he be Swich as e tellen Me', expressing a desire for more evidence than the knight can provide.[54] This desire to confirm the knight's account with his own eyes is also an addition to the English text, making Ypocras seek for truth through experience rather than through faith. If the knight's report is correct Ypocras intends to become Christ's disciple, while if Christ's skills are less impressive than described, he will make Christ his student.

The final instance of healing within the chapter, performed by Ypocras after he has heard of Christ's miracles, is substantially more ambiguous than previous examples or than its French source. The death of the king of Persia's son is presented only from the perspective of the people: first they 'wenden' that he was dead and then, after the cure, they 'seiden that this A fair Miracle was'.[55] They judge that Ypocras 'to god Aperede with Owten dowte'.[56] As the English text has shown its readers both true and false reports of dead patients and miraculous cures, it is notable that the details of the illness and the outcome are described at second hand. In contrast to the recovery of the emperor's nephew, at no point does the narrator here intervene to give a clear statement that the king's son was in fact alive. Most importantly, the English omits the test for life which appears in the French version. In the original Ypocras is almost convinced that the king's son is dead, but he finally detects breath in him by holding a wisp of wool in front of his nostrils. It is therefore clear both to Ypocras and to the reader that the boy is alive.[57] In the English, nothing demonstrates for certain that Ypocras is not confronted by a dead body: the boy is described as a 'theke Cors', which suggests death while not actually specifying it.[58] This new ambiguity introduced in Lovelich's version puts the reader in the position of those who view the miracle within the text, and are forced to discern between a miracle and a medical cure.

Susan Crane, in her comparison of insular and continental romances, argues that 'the English poets complement their removal of ironic perspectives with alterations designed to make their material less troubling and more open to understanding'.[59] Although her work focuses on earlier romances, written between the eleventh and the fourteenth centuries, it is clear that the standard form of adaptation she sees is not at play at least in this section of Lovelich's translation. Instead, Lovelich draws attention precisely to the ambiguity between medicine and miracle. While external context makes it clear to the reader that Christ and Ypocras are performing acts of different kinds, Lovelich's translation emphasizes the difficulty of observers in distinguishing natural from supernatural acts in cases where earthly medicine is able to produce such startling results.

Although recognizing that medical and miraculous cures stem from very different causes, Lovelich magnifies the status of earthly medicine by showing how marvellous its outcomes might be.

NOTES

1. Dorothy Kempe, *The Legend of the Holy Grail, its Sources, Character and Development: The Introduction to, and Part V of, Herry Lovelich's Verse 'History of the Holy Grail'*, Early English Text Society E.S. XCV, (London: Early English Text Society, 1905), p. v.
2. Robert W. Ackerman, 'Henry Lovelich's Name', *Modern Language Notes* 67 (1952) 531; George Kane, *Middle English Literature: A Critical Study of the Romances, the Religious Lyrics, Piers Plowman* (London: Methuen, 1951), p. 17.
3. Karl Heinz Göller, 'From Logres to Carbonek: The Arthuriad of Charles Williams', in *The Grail: A Casebook*, Arthurian Characters and Themes V, ed., Dhira B. Mahoney (New York: Garland, 2000), p. 128, n.28.
4. Roger Dalrymple, '"Evele knowen ye Merlyne, in certayne": Henry Lovelich's *Merlin*', in *Medieval Insular Romance: Translation and Innovation*, eds Judith Weiss, Jennifer Fellowes, and Morgan Dickson (Cambridge: D.S. Brewer, 2000), pp. 155-67; Raluca L. Radulescu, *Romance and its Contexts in Fifteenth-Century England: Politics, Piety and Penitence* (Cambridge: D.S. Brewer, 2013).
5. As the surviving manuscripts of the French *Graal* vary, it is difficult to identify Lovelich's exact source. I have consulted *The Vulgate Version of the Arthurian Romances: Volume I: Lestoire del Saint Graal*, ed. H. Oskar Sommer (Washington: The Carnegie Institution of Washington, 1909) and the translation in Carol J. Chase, trans., *Lancelot-Grail: The Old French Arthurian Vulgate and Post-Vulgate in Translation: I: The History of the Holy Grail*, gen. ed. Norris J. Lacy (Cambridge: D.S. Brewer, 2010), which includes variant readings from earlier editions by E. Hucher and Jean-Paul Ponceau. I have also consulted the manuscript copy in London, British Library, Additional MS 10292. Quotations will be given from Chase's translation.
6. Nancy G. Siraisi, *Medieval & Early Renaissance Medicine: An Introduction to Knowledge and Practice* (Chicago and London: U of Chicago P, 1990), pp. 65 and 71.
7. London, British Library, Sloane MS 6, fol. 175^v.
8. Ernest Wickersheimer, 'Légendes hippocratiques du Moyen Âge', *Sudhoffs Archiv für Geschichte der Medizin und der Naturwissenschaften* 45:2 (July 1961) 164-75.
9. '*Oh, quantos labores insumpserit hic Author, in rebus non ita probabilibus*', fol. iii^v. The manuscript is fully digitized at *Parker Library on the Web*, <https://parker.stanford.edu/parker> accessed 15 July 2019. The Ypocras section appears on fols 45^v-48^r.
10. Lovelich makes significant changes at this point. As they are not relevant to this article's broader theme of miracle and medicine, I discuss them here only briefly. In the English, the King of Persia gives Ypocras his daughter's hand in marriage. In the French, by contrast, Ypocras demands the twelve-year-old daughter of the King of Sur – barely of marriageable age under canon law – as a reward for his medical expertise. Both kings are clearly astonished at the request. The coerced marriage in the French provides some motivation for the wife's hatred of Ypocras, which in Lovelich's English is explained only by her sense that she has been married to someone beneath her status.
11. *The History of the Holy Grail, Englisht, Ab. 1450 A.D., by Herry Lonelich, Skynner, Part I*, ed. Frederick J. Furnivall, Early English Text Society E.S. XX/XXIV (London: Early English Text Society, 1874), ch. xxx, ll.32-3. The edition of the poem continues in *Part*

II (E.S. XXVIII/XXX, 1877). Quotations from the poem are cited by volume, chapter and line from this edition. The use of 'Lonelich' rather than 'Lovelich' in Furnivall's title is erroneous; see Ackerman, 'Lovelich's Name'.

12. *Holy Grail*, ed. Furnivall, II.xxxvi.627-9.
13. *Holy Grail*, ed. Furnivall, II.xxxvi.66.
14. *Holy Grail*, ed. Furnivall, II.xxxvi.73-4.
15. *Holy Grail*, ed. Furnivall, II.xxxvi.92.
16. *Holy Grail*, ed. Furnivall, II.xxxvi.93-4.
17. *Middle English Dictionary* 'areren', senses 4 and 6. <https://quod.lib.umich.edu/m/middle-english-dictionary/dictionary> accessed 20 July 2019.
18. *Holy Grail*, ed. Furnivall, II.xxxvi.108; 111-12.
19. *Holy Grail*, ed. Furnivall, II.xxxvi.113; 144.
20. Mary F. Wack, 'Lovesickness in "Troilus"', *Pacific Coast Philology* 19 (1984) 56.
21. *Holy Grail*, ed. Furnivall, p. 19.
22. Chase, trans., *Holy Grail*, p. 192.
23. *Holy Grail*, ed. Furnivall, II.xxxvi.242-4.
24. *Holy Grail*, ed. Furnivall, II.xxxvi.303-4.
25. *Holy Grail*, ed. Furnivall, II.xxxvi.333; 335.
26. '"wel Sire," thanne quod the Emperour, / "Sethen I may not Knowen of oure langour / [then] themperour forth wente Anon, / and Into his Chambre gan to gon.' *Holy Grail*, ed. Furnivall, II.xxxvi.371-6. The line numbering in Furnivall's edition appears to assume that two lines are missing here.
27. *Holy Grail*, ed. Furnivall, II.xxxvi.381-2.
28. *Holy Grail*, ed. Furnivall, II.xxxvi.310-12.
29. *Holy Grail*, ed. Furnivall, I.xv.236-7.
30. *Holy Grail*, ed. Furnivall, I.xvi.133-54.
31. *Holy Grail*, ed. Furnivall, I.xvii.119-142.
32. *Holy Grail*, ed. Furnivall, II.xxxviii.39-58; II.xliii.321-30; II.441-50.
33. *Holy Grail*, ed. Furnivall, II.lii.195-264.
34. *Holy Grail*, ed. Furnivall, II.xxxvi.3-6. Furnivall incorrectly prints 'that' instead of 'than' at the beginning of l.6.
35. Chase, trans., *Holy Grail*, p. 188.
36. *Holy Grail*, ed. Furnivall, II.xxxvi.10.
37. *Holy Grail*, ed. Furnivall, II.xxxvi.21; 30.
38. *Holy Grail*, ed. Furnivall, II.xxxvi.54.
39. *Holy Grail*, ed. Furnivall, II.xxxvi.57; Louise M. Bishop, *Words, Stones, and Herbs: The Healing Word in Medieval and Early Modern England* (Syracuse: Syracuse UP, 2007). The phrase is especially discussed in Chapter 3, pp. 77-101.
40. Chase, trans., *Holy Grail*, p. 190.
41. *Holy Grail*, ed. Furnivall, II.xxxvi.113; 144
42. Chase, trans., *Holy Grail*, p. 190.
43. Luke 8:41-42; 49-56.
44. *Holy Grail*, ed. Furnivall, II.xxxvi.148-50.
45. Although the miracles of the saints may not yet have happened within the timeline of the poem, the Old Testament miracles would have occurred. These include resurrections performed by Elijah (1 Kings 17:17-24) and Elisha, both before (2 Kings 4:18-27) and after (2 Kings 13:20-21) his death.
46. *Holy Grail*, ed. Furnivall, II.xxxvi.403.
47. *Holy Grail*, ed. Furnivall, II.xxxvi.6; 400.

48. Chase, trans., *Holy Grail*, p. 195.
49. *Holy Grail*, ed. Furnivall, II.xxxvi.421.
50. *Holy Grail*, ed. Furnivall, II.xxxvi.60.
51. *Holy Grail*, ed. Furnivall, II.xxxvi.422.
52. *Holy Grail*, ed. Furnivall, II.xxxvi.425.
53. *Holy Grail*, ed. Furnivall, II.xxxvi.10.
54. *Holy Grail*, ed. Furnivall, II.xxxvi.427-8.
55. *Holy Grail*, ed. Furnivall, II.xxxvi.454; 470.
56. *Holy Grail*, ed. Furnivall, II.xxxvi.480.
57. Chase, trans., *Holy Grail*, p. 196.
58. *Holy Grail*, ed. Furnivall, II.xxxvi.458.
59. Susan Crane, *Insular Romance: Politics, Faith, and Culture in Anglo-Norman and Middle English Literature* (Berkeley: U of California P, 1986) p. 221.

Midwives and Witches: Reproductive Health, Rights, and Development in Amma Darko's *The Housemaid*

VERONICA BARNSLEY

> Our umbilical cord is still buried in the rural environment. We are the very few that
> are exposed to Western education.   Flora Nwapa[1]

Amma Darko's novel *The Housemaid* (1998)[2] deals with the stark
economic challenges, tangled social networks, and ethical conundrums of
women's lives in contemporary Ghana. The novel's diverse cast of women
across generations 'kneads' together women's experiences in order to
express, as Darko herself puts it, 'some realities about Ghana'.[3] Sexual and
reproductive rights are denied, demanded, and interrogated in a text that
unashamedly does the 'work' of storytelling for which women writers in
Ghana have only recently been recognized.[4] In asserting that 'most African
writing has a social function', Darko presents her task as an urgent one.[5]
Along with Darko's other novels that address such topics as girls'
education, prostitution, and migration, *The Housemaid* falls into an unusual
category in the global literary marketplace. It is a novel written for African
(and specifically Ghanaian) readers that uses 'the storyteller function'
familiar in African narrative, and is sharply relevant to current thinking
about the relationship between postcolonial literatures, international
development, and global health.[6]

This article pays attention to the novel's representations of reproductive
rights and health with an awareness of the 'complex social and structural
forces' that Paul Farmer et al identify as crucial factors in global health.
These include 'poverty, inequality and environmental degradation' and
require 'a broad-based agenda of social change'.[7] An interdisciplinary
sociocultural or, as Farmer terms it, 'biosocial' approach to global health
is particularly pertinent in examining midwifery given that, as the above
epigraph from Nigerian writer, Flora Nwapa, indicates, birth practices are
not only vital to improving the health of women and children globally but
also have a figurative power within the sociocultural imagination of
nations and communities that is often overlooked.

While there is an abundance of critical commentary on representations of motherhood in African women's writing, isolating depictions of midwifery for analysis enables us to focus on the conceptual and material frictions between reproductive rights, development indicators (in this case chiefly maternal mortality rates and access to antenatal care), and diverse, even opposed, attitudes and practices relating to maternal and infant health.[8] This methodology is in tune with *The Housemaid*'s own articulation of the communal impetus of African discourses of rights, development, and health while avoiding neocolonial oversimplifications about African cultures collectively. It correlates with Sonia Corrêa et al's assertion that 'economic and social rights accruing to communities (for safe water, health care, livelihoods) are ultimately about the individual bodies that need these resources to live. Rights are always individual and social at the same time, just as persons are'.[9] In Darko's novel, traditions and practices relating to sex and birth are socially situated and are adaptable to local circumstances that are moulded by the pressures of global economics. Darko's representation of the difficulties of bridging socioeconomic divisions to attain rights for all within societies in the Global South maps onto the conceptual gap that Chi Chi Oke and Chimuroake O. Izugbara cogently define: 'understanding or interpreting rights in African settings within the framework defined by contemporary human rights discourse poses steep challenges to making progress in the realization of sexual and reproductive rights'.[10]

In addressing this issue, as Nwapa's statement implies and Darko herself has claimed, the work of the privileged African woman writer is partly to mediate between women in rural or marginalized communities and the national and international actors who aim to improve their lives. In dealing with the cross-cutting factors that affect reproductive rights and health, Darko ensures that readers encounter the 'socially embedded nature of reproductive agency' and recognize that, to use Andrea Cornwall's term, 'reproductive strategies' are 'always tempered by relations of sociality and power' in each specific setting, often frustrating interventionist development mindsets and binary assumptions separating urban and rural, 'traditional' and 'modern'.[11]

Umbilical politics and development

The Housemaid begins with a neonatal death that could well be a statistic in global health data. Sustainable Development Goal 3 (Good Health and Well Being) identifies child and maternal health as a priority and aims to reduce the global maternal mortality ratio to fewer than 70 per 100,000 live births, and end preventable deaths of newborns and children under 5 years of age by 2030. Low and middle income countries (LMICs) accounted for approximately 99% (302,000) of the global maternal deaths in 2015, with roughly 66% in sub-Saharan Africa.[12] In Ghana, significant improvements have been made. Nevertheless the WHO classified the country as making 'insufficient' progress by 2015, when its maternal mortality rate (MMR) measured 319 per 100,000 live births in comparison to the global rate of 216. 70.6% of births were assisted by a skilled birth attendant (SBA) but with large disparities in the extent and quality of service between urban and rural locations.

In *The Housemaid*, the discovery of 'the gruesome, decaying corpse of a newborn baby girl' on the outskirts of a remote northern village introduces a compressed and fast-moving narrative that addresses such urban-rural disparities by detailing the manipulation and deception that leads to a young rural mother abandoning the body of the child she conceived while she was working in the city.[13] While Part One of the text introduces touches of crime fiction in setting up the mystery of the child's death, by Part Two we are aware that the narrative has a more sociological focus in anatomizing the factors that lead to the denouement. Efia, the housemaid of the title, is revealed to be the teenage mother being vilified in the press by headlines including 'MOTHERHOOD ON TRIAL!' and on the street in a cacophony of opinions ranging from those of misogynist truck drivers – 'when the mother is caught, her womb should be removed' – to feminist street vendors – 'why do you men make nonsense of such issues, to escape blame?'[14] This noisy reportage silences Efia within her own story. She becomes the virtually voiceless centre of a narrative in which her life has become public property, and we later learn the extent to which she has been manipulated for private gain (albeit that of her own family). Efia's grandmother has orchestrated a plot to gain wealth by encouraging her granddaughter to become pregnant and to blackmail her employer to take on the child, thereby ensuring an inheritance for the family. This is presented as their right given that Tika, the wealthy young woman who employs Efia in the capital Accra, is related to the family and wishes to maintain a link with her roots in the village of Kataso.

Tika is a vocal and volatile businesswoman who nevertheless shares with her maid and the other poor young women in the text (Akua, a porter and street child who migrates from Kataso to the city of Kumasi, and Bibio, the daughter of a fish hawker) the frustration and disappointment produced by an unequal regime of gender:

It had never been Tika's dream to be single and childless at the ripe old age of thirty-five. Living only with Efia, her maid, in a two-room estate house, and travelling frequently all over Africa to scout for goods to sell in Ghana, was not much fun. Neither was hopping into bed with men of all shapes and sizes for the flimsiest of business excuses.[15]

Tika and Efia are both driven to use sex to get closer to their economic goals. This is a strategy exemplified across the economic scale by Tika's mother, the rich and mercenary Sekiywa, and by the shrewd street child, Akua. The relationship between sex and money becomes more various and complex when we begin to analyse reproductive politics. Tika both trades sex for favours and aborts her illegitimate child to punish her mother for her neglect and bullying of Tika's late father. Tika's infertility following complications with the abortion recapitulates the situation of her father's first wife whom he divorced because she couldn't bear children. Although she is tempted to treat her situation as 'fate' given her familial history, Tika's narrative exemplifies the contingent factors at work in reproductive choices; she seizes her reproductive rights by choosing an abortion while using sex-for-money to maintain financial independence. Efia's pregnancy is also instrumental in her grasping after a better future through the means of using her baby as a bargaining tool for financial gain. Both women deliberately reject motherhood as a woman's fulfilment and purpose. Efia's family cannot afford to bring up a child – 'For poor people like us, sometimes certain situations are worse than death', Efia's mother explains – and Tika fears that she will replicate her mother's neglectful parenting.[16]

Between these two women at opposite ends of the economic spectrum moves *The Housemaid*'s mediator figure, who is the only character without a name besides the baby, and who is known simply as Teacher. She negotiates a way forward after Efia's blackmail is revealed, though she is unable to prevent the crisis leading to the child's death. Her actions are not entirely altruistic; she receives remuneration in the form of 'cassavas and plantains and bushmeat' for her services and appreciates the social status she gains in her home village.[17] However, her educated, translocal and unattached position enables her to operate as a sounding board for Tika and a saviour for Efia. While both Tika and Teacher grew up in the capital, Teacher is 'one of the few Katasoans in Accra with formal jobs and the comfort of a home, one of whom had been Tika's father'.[18] The attitudes and behaviours of these two influential women in the text are contrasted through a comparison of their births:

Her [Teacher's] feelings for Kataso never waned. This was because, like Tika's father, she had been born inside a traditional midwife's hut in the village, and her umbilical cord had been placed in a calabash and buried by her grandmother in the brown earth of the village. Tika, in contrast, was delivered in a hospital in the city and had had her umbilical cord flushed down into the sewerage system with countless others.[19]

Here the ancestral connection to the village is presented as underpinning a sense of security and purpose for Teacher that in Tika's case has been harshly severed at the hands of modern obstetrics.[20] By voicing the natal distinction between Tika and Teacher through the fleshly signifier of the umbilical cord, the text refuses to define exactly *who* maintains the view that midwifery practices can define your relation to home and community. However, the image of multiple umbilical cords populating the sewerage system reimagines the urban masses not only in terms of bodily waste, as is frequently the case in postcolonial narratives of precarious city living, but also in terms of a loss of personal and social connection when separated from the implicitly fertile 'brown earth' of the village.[21] This passage also homes in on an irony of neoliberal development that the novel raises and that has been recognized in feminist critiques of development: overt commitments to making women the target of development initiatives can be more about the attractiveness of gender as a 'technocratic category' than about achieving 'gender justice'.[22] This certainly applies to Tika, who reaps the benefits of modern healthcare but is caught within a dehumanizing and exploitative socioeconomic structure. Efia, an unequivocal victim of the system that partially benefits Tika, has access neither to abortion nor antenatal care, and gives birth while living on the streets out of fear of both medical professionals and her own family.

The unceremonious severing and disposal of her umbilical cord not only represents Tika's position as the child of a rural migrant to the city who feels like she has lost her heritage but also prefigures her grief when her first love, Owuraku, abandons her. Owuraku's belief that love is about more than money is implicitly connected to the privilege of education that neither of Tika's parents possessed, and it is a stipulation that she unknowingly violates in seeking to provide for *his* education and *their* shared future through her business. Tika's lack of compunction in trading sex to secure this future is linked via the umbilical cord trope to a depersonalized and industrialized birth story that she shares with all Ghanaian women receiving skilled antenatal care in a modern facility. Ama de-Graft Atkins and Kwadwo Koram note that the Ghanaian healthcare system has always been pluralistic with traditional medical practitioners, missions, and NGOs being important players. However the user-fee health services of the 1990s meant 'catastrophic health expenditure' for the poor and a failure of the state to get any closer to the provision of equitable healthcare.[23] Given this context, Tika is one of few able to afford an abortion, but her very exceptionality demonstrates that the ethical standards that Owuraku espouses in relation to the privacy and intimacy of sex and reproduction are rarely achievable: 'He was a university graduate with pride and prospects. For Owuraku, money was good, but not at any price. And that was a point Tika had missed.'[24] Tika misses the point because she has grown up asking her mother, 'So when you finish making money will you play with me?' and being told by actions as much as words that financial profit takes precedence over (and indeed pays for) both childcare and education.[25] Healthcare is another commodity that Tika and her mother can buy but is not one that, in this era of structural adjustment in Africa, is available to all.

In Teacher's case, the explanatory form in the quotation above – 'this was because'– presents her social and emotional connection to Kataso as naturalized due to the correct rituals being performed at her birth. However, this belies the fact that the material conditions in the village mediate against exactly the financial security and successful social connections that Teacher achieves: 'The young men ... left for Accra, Kumasi and Takoradi, to work as shoe-shine boys, truck pushers or hawkers', while for the young women the choice is to stay and marry in extreme poverty or to 'work as housemaids and babysitters' in the city 'though many ended up as iced water sellers or prostitutes'.[26] Teacher is an exception, having 'got to where she did because she was adopted by a relation who was married to a man from Accra'.[27] She is put through school by her relation's husband and gains the qualifications that Tika fails to achieve. Teacher pays for her benefits by securing a start in the workplace for girls from Kataso; in the case of Efia, for example, when she has completed four years' service Teacher will send her to be trained as a seamstress. Teacher therefore functions to contrast traditional beliefs that community is defined by ritual and inheritance with the more haphazard and risky connections acquired in the city. She also draws attention to the post-structural adjustment situation in which the poor have been left 'bereft of government support, and the neoliberal shibboleth that the unfettered market can and will sort out all human needs has disastrously fallen on its face'.[28]

The novel's critique of neoliberal healthcare policies comes to the fore when we focus on the figure of the midwife. Whether in her hut or in a hospital, she not only provides for a safe birth but is also a gatekeeper of social opportunities. Around her, myths have evolved (such as the ritual burying of the umbilical cord) that could, the novel suggests, potentially challenge the instrumentalist understanding of development as primarily defined and measured by the economic aims of international institutions, notably the World Bank and the IMF.[29] The midwife's absence can lead, as we have seen in the case of Efia, to physical and psychological distress and even death, but her presence provides for more than medical needs. Midwifery practices can define how a woman views herself and how she is viewed by others, but operate according to gendered socioeconomic factors. In the case of Efia, the primary issue is not the availability of antenatal care but rather the social, cultural, and economic barriers to accessing it. Efia stands between the more 'developed' axes of Tika and Teacher (one rich and one educated), posing an open question about how reproductive rights can be made to work for women. At the plot's finale, when the deception of Efia's family is revealed and Tika realizes her own culpability in the 'web of deceit', Tika and Teacher become indistinguishable – 'together, they laughed and cried; laughing and crying away their pain, their disappointment, their anger, their fear. And laughing with hope'.[30]

In the radical togetherness of these childless women, the novel can be read as exposing the inadequacy of development initiatives that focus on changing women's behaviours to improve reproductive health on the assumption that 'poverty is less of a structural issue, and more of a personal and maternal issue'.[31] Its representation of women who gamble their reproductive chips, as Tika and Efia do, makes it clear that neither market economics (in Tika's case) nor the improved availability of maternity services (in Efia's) guarantees improvements in maternal and infant health. These women's difficulties provoke us to interrogate both rights-based and policy-driven approaches to development in Africa. On the one hand, I read the novel as articulating Oke and Izugbara's argument that modern human rights declarations, founded on the idea that all human beings are born free and equal, lack 'grounding in the lived and dynamic, everyday social experiences of the people' existing on the underside of globalization, such as Efia and her family.[32] On the other hand, by equating modern midwifery with the anonymity of neoliberal production (and waste) and traditional midwifery with the creation of more surplus rural labourers, the text can also be mobilized to critique policy-based approaches which use 'the discourse of efficiency, effectiveness and value for money' to promote improvements in maternal and infant health.[33] At the very least, the novel suggests, effective development must take into account the longevity and adaptability of customs and traditions focused on sexuality, gender, and the body, and promote community-driven improvements in healthcare.[34] In the next section I consider in more detail how Darko navigates these development challenges stylistically and point to insights that *The Housemaid* offers into the 'social location' of reproductive rights by examining the function of the midwife in relation to her feared counterpoint, the witch.[35]

Midwives, witches, and grandmothers

Women who fail in waging the 'desperate war for economic survival' and who are 'forsaken and forgotten' by their families risk being pronounced witches in Darko's Ghana.[36] At the end of their reproductive lives, they, like Efia at the beginning of hers, are publicly vilified. The novel draws upon actual incidents and press reports in charting the rapid decline of female fortunes in its opening portrait.

> A dejected widow, once upon a time a vibrant akpeteshie seller in the village of Braha, now penniless, aged and lonesome, started towards 'witchdom' when one of her grandchildren developed kwashiorkor. She had turned herself into a snake and lodged inside the poor child's stomach, they said.[37]

It is this unfortunate woman, driven to the outskirts of the village, who demands the search that leads to the body of Efia's newborn being found. The narrative's circularity (the return to the site/sight of its own beginning in the discovery of the dead baby) establishes how women are ensnared within a matrix of deprivation. In the trajectory the novel traces from birth to death the umbilical cord secures a woman to her community, but ageing, poverty, and the perniciousness of the gods can mean that that community, severs ties with her when she is at her most vulnerable. Whether it is Efia with her secure village connections or Tika with her urban provenance who is more impacted by these ideologies of birth and ageing is open to debate. It is clear, however, that neither rights-based approaches to improving reproductive health nor policy-driven initiatives will easily be able to intervene in entrenched psychosocial, cultural, and spiritual perceptions of birth and ageing. It is the sardonic storyteller, surely a village insider and yet at a remove from the action in both intellectual and geographical terms, who makes use of 'once upon a time' to convert the quotidian information about the widow into a potentially moral discourse that speaks back both to the 'they' who pronounce her a witch and the 'they' outside Ghana who form a large segment of Darko's readers.

The stance of the storyteller gives a gravitas to the marginal lives she narrates. The democratic reflexivity of this insistent but for the most part unobtrusive narrative voice is created by amalgamating fictional modes, including social realism, folktale, and the orature that is a hallmark of West African literature, particularly in the well-known Ananse stories. As Stephanie Newell observes, West African orality is multidimensional and responsive, often marrying current affairs with historical or moral narratives and eliciting audience participation.[38] Occasionally Darko's narrator comments on a character's perceptions – 'Efia was no fool' – but, with the exception of Tika who is granted more psychological airtime, motivations and opinions are not extensively explored.[39] The text's complexity comes about through the positioning of characters in counterpoint to expose each other's flaws and articulate social and familial conflict. A raft of minor characters voice alternative scenarios on the main themes, the most notable example being Mami Korkor and her daughter Bibio whose spats over the requirement that the daughter 'play mother' to her siblings elaborate on the 'pathetic life' of poor girls.[40] Cynthia Ward's response to Buchi Emecheta's *The Joys of Motherhood* (1979), a novel which also deals with reproductive health, is relevant here. She argues that in narratives that maintain 'a fidelity to the oral', the 'essentially untextualizable' voices and meanings of women take precedence over 'the putative political and historical hegemony' of the written word (that, in literal terms, many of Darko's characters do not have access to).[41]

Within this multivocal framework the witch and the midwife have heterogenous figurative possibilities. The witch as a social outcast operates as the negative face of old age, in haunting opposition to the grandmother figure, with the added complication that Efia's grandmother's behaviour is witchlike *despite* her central position in the family. The proximity between the two is clear as the grandmother functions to orchestrate and endorse the family's decisions but always with the threat, established from the novel's opening, that her authority will be turned against her. Her vicious plotting and exaggerated physical and emotional performance of poverty combines the worst of both urban and rural worlds in a parody of capitalist economics in which 'sweet cash' must be sought whatever the risks.[42]

In contrast to the grandmother/witch's centrality to the novel's theme and plot and association with death, midwives, who usher in life, are peripheral to the narrative but, as we have seen, are essential in reinforcing cultural traditions and social bonds. This role of midwifery is clear in the introduction provided to Kataso.

> Kataso, a village in the Eastern hills, had no flowing water, no electricity, no entertainment centre, nothing ...Which therefore left sex as the only really affordable entertainment in Kataso. Everyone – young, old, mature and immature – indulged in it freely, making the two midwives the busiest village professionals.[43]

The reference to the 'two midwives' as 'professionals' points us nimbly towards the need for a framework for understanding health that is specific to the local context. The midwives are undoubtedly traditional birth attendants (TBAs) and their methods, likely to include praying, revelations, and herbal medicine, would not satisfy the standards of modern obstetric services.[44] Yet as global health research on TBAs indicates, they are likely to be accessible, affordable, and essential to the functioning of a successful community health system.[45] As Stacy Leigh Pigg points out, the words '"traditional birth attendant" serve as a placeholder, a blank waiting to be filled in at the local level where primary healthcare is to be carried out' and it is only by engaging with the cultural as well as the physiological aspects of pregnancy and birth that their roles can be understood.[46] Since the 1970s the World Health Organization has recognized the value and necessity of engaging with TBAs to improve maternal and infant health. In Ghana these efforts have proven essential in the Safe motherhood programme introduced in 1987.[47] There is also a concern, as Pigg discusses, that monitoring and intervening in local healthcare practices can fracture or marginalize sociocultural realities deemed 'traditional', presenting 'modern' medicine as the 'locus of authoritative knowledge'.[48] In *The Housemaid*, traditional midwives are figures of aspiration in their own right and, given the lack of family planning, occupy financially lucrative positions. Throughout the novel there is a sense that trust and an understanding of the benefits of antenatal care are vital in encouraging women to seek care.[49]

Like Teacher, who straddles the divide between illiterate poverty and educated wealth, midwives have the potential to mediate between traditional medical practices and modern biomedical approaches. Darko's narrative seems to suggest that the potential for skilled birth attendants to impact the health and wellbeing of rural women has yet to be fully tapped, as has the figurative capacity of the midwife to capture women's translocal, transitional experiences of modernity in the Global South. Again, Efia is caught in the middle, fearing both midwives and witches. For Efia and her peers in Accra, midwives are perceived as a potential threat to the autonomy of girls inhabiting the city's slums and working in the informal economy. Although her friends are concerned – 'You'll have to insist she sees a midwife. Her stomach has stopped growing' – Efia refuses to visit any care professional as she believes she may be arrested for stealing from Tika.[50] Yet, on returning to the village, Efia fears the consequences of failing to perform the requisite rituals over her baby's corpse to appease the wrath of the ancestors invoked by her grandmother. Midwifery, then, operates both discursively and in practice as a field through which we can begin to see how reproductive rights and health can be determined by competing local sociocultural practices, especially in communities with sparse educational and healthcare provision. By placing disparate social constructions of midwifery and birth in interaction with each other without privileging a singular perspective the novel opens up a dialogue on the contingency of 'reproductive strategies'.

The viewpoint that is hardest to sympathize with in *The Housemaid* is that of the grandmother. As Naana Banyiwa Horne points out, she is 'possibly the most perplexing portrait of this figure in Ghanaian literature'.[51] Horne identifies three prototypes for grandmothers in African literature – the sage, the muse, and the crone – and argues that Efia's grandmother is so formidable because she combines and switches between these roles, cajoling, threatening, promising wealth then meting out punishment. Her revenge ploy invokes the ghost of Tika's father who 'wants to return to his family all that his evil wife stole from him' as well as taking advantage of matrilineal inheritance; if Tika adopts the baby, Efia will receive wealth that will then trickle down through the village.[52] The grandmother takes over the role of head of the family (an easy coup as Efia's father is an ineffectual drunkard) and performs the rituals that are men's prerogative. Her violation of kinship and community structures with her unabashed pursuit of wealth has its own trickle-down effect, making other women realize with discomfort that they are forced to sell their bodies (either in poorly paid labour or as sex objects) in order to participate in the neoliberal economic system that cares nothing for ritual or moral cleanliness. When she challenges her son-in-law for spiritual and social control he tells her:

> 'I'm going behind the hut right now, you old witch, to call upon the gods to reverse whatever it was you asked them. Do you hear me?' But the old lady grew even more defiant, 'Go ahead!' she shot back. 'Go and pour your libation. Who says the gods will favour a drunkard over a woman?'[53]

Both parties, however, are proven impotent in their attempts to exercise authority as the plan to dupe Tika is foiled by paternity testing. Nsorwhe, the lover whom Efia accuses of raping and impregnating her, reveals to Tika that he cannot father children and his demand for the test prompts Efia to run away. By including the back story that Nsorwhe has two children through his wife's infidelities, Darko makes clear that the babies of the middle classes are bargaining chips just as those of the poor are. This also holds true in the case of Tika's father who is lured away from his first wife by Sekyiwa's pregnancy. In both cases, bearing children is the extension of selling sex; a way for women to get ahead in the absence of educational and employment opportunities. Even in Tika's case, bearing Oruwakwu's child (or a child he believes to be his) could have legitimated her claim on him despite her disappointment at failing to pass her exams.

The grandmother's influence is clearly a destructive one that brings these exploitative patterns to the surface but, in placing her as central to the sexual and reproductive politics in her community, the text makes the point that improving women's lives in both economic and reproductive terms must include engaging not only with midwives and healthcare providers but with extended family and community networks, particularly elders. As Gupta et al demonstrate, '[g]randmothers may also serve as gatekeepers for health-seeking behaviour, especially with regard to their daughters and daughters-in-law'.[54] Even as it condemns an economic system that crushes the poor, the novel thereby asserts the adaptability of social bonds (primarily between women) and cultural practices. Darko's text shows us that reproductive rights (whether rhetorically and legally framed as such or not) are essential building blocks of social change and global health equity.[55]

In opposition to the grandmother's divisive influence, Tika's abortion and hysterectomy mark a new kind of transition into womanhood, one that challenges rural matrilineal authority and tentatively opens up the potential for women to counter the exploitative use of sex and the violation of reproductive freedoms. It also challenges the ubiquitous image of the African woman who is the 'target' or 'beneficiary' of development interventions – 'always poor, powerless and invariably pregnant'.[56] Tika's ultimate generosity towards Efia and her realization that both of them have been exploited by their rural relatives and urban labour relations stand in reflexive relation to the irredeemable outcome of Efia's pregnancy. From Tika's reproductive and sexual choices to Teacher's work to empower rural girls to Akua urging Efia to seek antenatal care and Bibio's angry formulation of girls' lack of opportunity, the characters demand, via the radical commitment of the storyteller, that their rights be instrumental in negotiating what Corrêa et al call 'the brave new worlds of "sex" and gender' that are 'triggered by markets and embedded in consumerism and commodification'.[57]

The only figure excluded from this fragile potential for community-driven rights bearing development is the disabled child. The open-ended dialogic storytelling in this case works to avoid any overt exploration of disability as a concern of either development or global health. It is the baby's condition, Down's Syndrome, rather than her death, that correlates in Efia's mind to the belief that a curse has been pronounced on her by Tika. In this case, the witch trope migrates to the city via Tika's genealogical connection to Kataso and finds root in Efia's disturbed mental state. There are doubts sprinkled through the text as to the strength of Efia's belief in her grandmother's superstitions. Nevertheless, her silent capitulation to her mother's and grandmother's demands yields nothing to speculation. Teacher explains the extreme reaction that would have resulted from the birth of a disabled child in the village:

> Had the baby been delivered in the village Kataso would have been thrown into a frenzied orgy of witch hunting. And only god knows how many poor lonely old widows would have been spared. So we can thank God not only that Efia did not give birth in Kataso, but also that the remains were found in a state beyond identifying it as having Down's.[58]

Efia's reluctance to speak is paralleled here by the reticence of the narrator whose forensic examination of sex and reproduction in Ghanaian society leaves a gap that would indicate that disability might be the next taboo to be tackled. It is worth noting that the two crucial moments in the text involve reproductive decisions that do not lead to live births; Tika's abortion and the death of Efia's neonate (indirectly attributable to her refusing antenatal care) and both usher in an examination of corruption and the failure of healthcare, education, and social justice (in relation to the street children particularly) within the framework of neoliberal economics. It must be admitted, however, that the novel's scrutiny stops short of examining either disability or illness as *lived* experiences. The association of Down's syndrome as well as other illnesses with witchcraft implies that in rehabilitating the widow from her designation as witch, Darko is also directing us towards another route not yet taken in Ghanaian fiction: disability and illness must also be delinked from witchcraft and imagined in the materialist and social constructionist terms in which the text presents gender, reproduction, and sexuality.

Conclusion

The superstition, trickery, and ruthlessness of *The Housemaid*'s intergenerational cast of characters verges on the grotesque in order to play out a moral drama where the only real loser is the disabled child of a poor teenage mother. The textual framework is one of sociological exploration and narratological diversion; the characters embark on a journey in which everyone, even Efia's feckless father and the big-hearted Nsorwe, plays their part and Efia does not end up being imprisoned or cast out. This collective focus enabled by the storyteller, and the attention given to the social forces that define the choices of individuals, provide an implicit critique of 'instrumentalised ideas of economic and political participation reduced to buzzwords that garland policy discourses'.[59] There are no humanitarian saviours and no ethical exceptions in Darko's text. All the characters exhibit desirous or manipulative behaviour to some degree, explicitly acknowledging their dependence on the global economic system while behaving in ways that testify to the lack of effective support from either the state or development agencies in meeting their needs and aspirations.

In a sense, then, *The Housemaid* is most valuable for what it does not do; it does not present either successful or failed development scenarios but rather captures uneven transitions and conflicts in socioeconomic and gender relations, articulating questions about reproductive rights, health, and development in a nonconfrontational but critical mode. On one level the text's social mission enables women 'to recognise, through dialogue and confrontation, the signs of their oppression and to react against them'.[60] And yet the silenced figures at its centre, the housemaid and her baby, remain as evidence of development's limitations in extricating the poor from the 'web of deceit' spun by structural forces and neoliberal rhetoric in order to deliver on the promise of reproductive rights and equitable healthcare.

NOTES

1. Flora Nwapa, 'Women and Creative Writing in Africa', in *African Literature: An Anthology of Criticism and Theory*, eds, Tejumola Olaniyan and Ato Quayson (London: Blackwell, 2007), pp. 526-32, p. 530.
2. Amma Darko, *The Housemaid* (Harlow: Heinemann, 1998).
3. Mary Ellen Higgins, 'Creating an Alternative Library: Amma Darko Interviewed by Ellie Higgins', *Journal of Commonwealth Literature*, 39:2 (2003) 111-20, p. 120.
4. Higgins notes that Darko is considered alongside 'Ghana's most remarkable women writers', Ama Ata Aidoo and Efua Sutherland. Higgins, 'Creating an Alternative Library', p. 111.
5. Higgins, 'Creating an Alternative Library', p. 115.

6. Madhu Krishnan, 'The Storyteller Function in Contemporary Nigerian Narrative', *The Journal of Commonwealth Literature*, 49:1 (2014) 29-45.

7. Paul Farmer, Jim Yong Kim, Arthur Kleinman and Matthew Basilico, 'Introduction: A Biosocial Approach to Global Health', in *Reimagining Global Health: An Introduction*, eds, Paul Farmer, Jim Yong Kim, Arthur Kleinman and Matthew Basilico (Berkeley: U of California P, 2013), pp. 1-15, p. 10.

8. On motherhood see Obioma Nnaemeka, ed., *The Politics of (M)othering: Womanhood, Identity, and Resistance in African Literature* (London: Routledge, 1997).

9. Sonia Corrêa, Rosalind Petchesky, and Richard Parker, *Sexuality, Health and Human Rights* (New York: Routledge, 2008), p. 2.

10. Chi Chi Oke and Chimuroake O. Izugbara, 'Unpacking Rights in Indigenous African Societies: Indigenous Culture and the Question of Sexual and Reproductive Rights in Africa', *BMC International Health and Human Rights*, 11 (Suppl 3): S2 (2011) 1-11, p. 1.

11. Andrea Cornwall, 'Taking Chances, Making Choices: The Tactical Dimensions of "Reproductive Strategies" in Southwestern Nigeria', *Med Anthropol* 26 (2007) 229-54, p. 252; cited in Oke and Izugbara, 'Unpacking Rights', p. 7. See also Kwame Gyekye, *Tradition and Modernity: Philosophical Reflections on the African Experience* (Philadelphia: Temple UP, 1997), Chapter 8, for a discussion of tradition and modernity.

12. World Health Organisation, UNICEF, UNFPA et al., 'Trends in Maternal Mortality' (2015), <https://www.who.int/reproductivehealth/publications/monitoring/maternal-mortality-2015/en/>.

13. Darko, *The Housemaid*, p. 4.

14. Darko, *The Housemaid*, p. 5.

15. Darko, *The Housemaid*, p. 14.

16. Darko, *The Housemaid*, p. 65.

17. Darko, *The Housemaid*, p. 56.

18. Darko, *The Housemaid*, p. 34.

19. Darko, *The Housemaid*, p. 35.

20. Lydia Aziato and Cephas N. Omenyo confirm that 'TBAs delay cutting of the cord [sic] and disposal of the placenta was associated with beliefs which indicated that when not properly disposed, it will have negative consequences on the child during adulthood.' 'Initiation of Traditional Birth Attendants and Their Traditional and Spiritual Practices during Pregnancy and Childbirth in Ghana', *BMC Pregnancy and Childbirth*, 18:64 (2018) 1-10, p. 1.

21. For example, see Michael K. Walonen, *Contemporary World Narrative Fiction and the Spaces of Neoliberalism* (London: Palgrave, 2016), Chapter 4.

22. Andrea Cornwall, Elizabeth Harrison and Ann Whitehead, 'Introduction', in *Feminisms in Development: Contradictions, Contestations and Challenges*, eds, Andrea Cornwall, Elizabeth Harrison and Ann Whitehead (London: Zed Books, 2007), pp. 1-20, p. 3.

23. Ama de-Graft Atkins and Kwadwo A. Koram, 'Health and Healthcare in Ghana, 1957–2017', in *The Economy of Ghana: Sixty Years After Independence,* eds, Ernest Aryeetey and Ravi Kanbur (Oxford: Oxford UP, 2017), pp. 365-84, p. 375.

24. Darko, *The Housemaid*, p. 24.

25. Darko, *The Housemaid*, p. 20.

26. Darko, *The Housemaid*, p. 29.

27. Darko, *The Housemaid*, p. 34.

28. Walonen, *Contemporary World Narrative Fiction*, p. 80.

29. See Sophie Bessis, 'The World Bank and Women: "Instrumental Feminism"', in *Eye*

to Eye: Women Practising Development Across Cultures, eds, Susan Perry and Celeste Schenck (London: Zed Books, 2001), pp. 10-24.

30. Darko, *The Housemaid*, p. 107.
31. Helen Penn, 'The Rhetoric and Realities of Early Childhood Programmes Promoted by the World Bank', in *Childhoods at the Intersection of the Local and the Global,* eds, Afua Twum-Danso Imoh and Robert Ame (London: Palgrave, 2010), pp. 75-94, p. 80.
32. Oke and Izugbara, 'Unpacking Rights', p. 3.
33. Fenella Porter, 'Gender Equality and the Discursive Landscape of Non-governmental Action in Development: The Inevitable Failure of International NGOs to Represent the Interests of Women?', in *Handbook on Development and Social Change,* eds, G. Honor Fagan and Ronaldo Munck (Cheltenham: Edward Elgar, 2018), pp. 395-413, p. 396. When using the terms 'modern' and 'traditional' I recognize the epistemological problems with the term 'traditional' that Stacy Leigh Pigg discusses, particularly the notion that it is an empty signifier. See Pigg, 'Authority in Translation: Finding, Knowing, Naming, and Training "Traditional Birth Attendants" in Nepal', in *Childbirth and Authoritative Knowledge,* eds, Robbie Davis-Floyd and Carolyn Sargent (Berkeley: U of California P, 1997), pp. 233-62. However, the term 'traditional' has also been politicized in opposition to 'modern midwife' in some contexts, particularly Latin America and the Caribbean. In global health research 'traditional' midwives are usually known as traditional birth attendants (TBAs). In *The Housemaid* the term 'midwife' is used for all birth attendants regardless of qualifications.
34. Oke and Izugbara, 'Unpacking Rights', p. 3.
35. Oke and Izugbara, 'Unpacking Rights', p. 10.
36. Darko, *The Housemaid*, p. 3.
37. Darko, *The Housemaid*, p. 3. Akpeteshie is the national spirit of Ghana, produced by distilling palm wine or sugar cane. Kwashiorkor is a form of malnutrition caused by a lack of protein and typically found in young children.
38. Stephanie Newell, *West African Literatures: Ways of Reading* (Oxford: Oxford UP, 2006), pp. 59-61.
39. Darko, *The Housemaid*, p. 49.
40. Darko, *The Housemaid*, p. 11.
41. Cynthia Ward, 'What They Told Buchi Emecheta: Oral Subjectivity and the Joys of "Otherhood"', *PMLA* 105:1 (1990) 83–97.
42. Darko, *The Housemaid*, p. 3.
43. Darko, *The Housemaid*, p. 29.
44. For a discussion of the initiation and methods of TBAs and their role and training in the modern healthcare system, see Aziato and Omenyo, 'Initiation of Traditional Birth Attendants'.
45. See S. Itina, 'Characteristics of Traditional Birth Attendants and Their Beliefs and Practices in the Offot Clan, Nigeria', *Bulletin of the World Health Organization,* 75:6 (1997) 563–67.
46. Pigg, 'Authority in Translation', p. 239.
47. World Health Organization, *Traditional Birth Attendants: A Joint WHO/UNFPA/UNICEF Statement* (Geneva: WHO, 1992), <http:// apps.who.int/iris/bitstream/10665/38994/1/9241561505.pdf>, p. 18.
48. Pigg, 'Authority in Translation', p. 233.
49. This chimes with the findings of C.A. Eades et al. that in rural Ghana traditional midwives are frequently preferred by women due to their accessibility and familiarity, often sharing beliefs and values with their clients. C.A. Eades et al., 'Traditional Birth Attendants and Maternal Mortality in Ghana', *Soc. Sci. Med.* 36:11 (1993) 1503-1507,

p. 1505. See also Itina, 'Characteristics of Traditional Birth Attendants'.

50. Darko, *The Housemaid*, p. 97.

51. Naana Banyiwa Horne, 'Sage, Muse, Crone: The Grandmother in Amma Darko's Novels', *Broadening the Horizon: Critical Introductions to Amma Darko*, ed., Vincent O. Odamtten (Banbury: Ayebia Clarke, 2007), pp. 111-34, p. 119.

52. Darko, *The Housemaid*, p. 46.

53. Darko, *The Housemaid*, p. 73.

54. Mira L. Gupta, Raymond Akawire Aborigo, Philip Baba Adongo et al., 'Grandmothers as Gatekeepers? The Role of Grandmothers in Influencing Health-seeking for Mothers and Newborns in Rural Northern Ghana', *Global Public Health*, 10:9 (2015) 1078-91, p. 1078.

55. Farmer et al., *Reimagining Global Health*, p. 309.

56. Everjoice J. Win, 'Not Very Poor, Powerless or Pregnant: The African Woman Forgotten by Development', in *Feminisms in Development: Contradictions, Contestations and Challenges*, eds, Andrea Cornwall and Elizabeth Harrison (London: Zed Books, 2007), pp. 79-85, p. 79.

57. Corrêa et al., *Sexuality, Health and Human Rights*, p. 23.

58. Darko, *The Housemaid*, p. 102.

59. Andrea Cornwall and Althea-Maria Rivas, 'From "Gender Equality" and "Women's Empowerment" to Global Justice: Reclaiming a Transformative Agenda for Gender and Development', *Third World Quarterly*, 36 (2) 396-415, cited in Porter, 'Gender Equality', p. 395.

60. Monica Bungaro, 'Victims and/or Victimisers? Women's De(Con)structive Power in *The Housemaid*', in *Broadening the Horizon*, ed., Odamtten, pp. 28-47, p. 45.

KATHY JETÑIL-KIJINER

Monster

Sometimes I wonder if Marshallese women are the chosen ones.

I wonder if someone selected us from a stack. Drew us out slow. Methodical. Then, issued the order:

Give birth to nightmares. Show the world what happens. When the sun explodes inside you.

How many stories of nuclear war are hidden in our bodies?

574 – the number of stillbirths and miscarriages after the bombs of 1951. Before the bombs? 52.

Bella Compoj told the UN she could no longer have children. That she saw her friends give birth to ugly things.

Nerik gave birth to something resembling the eggs of a sea turtle and Flora gave birth to something like the intestines[1]

She told this to a committee of men who washed their hands of this sin – these women who bore unholy things – created from exploding spit and ugly things.

And how these women buried their nightmares. Beneath a coconut tree. Pretended it never happened. Sinister. Hideous. Monster. More jellyfish than child.

And yet. They could see the chest inhale. Exhale. Could it be

human?

Nerik gave birth to something resembling the eggs of a sea turtle and Flora gave birth to something like intestines.

In our legends lives a monster. Mejenkwaad. Woman demons – unhinged jaws swallowing canoes, men, babies. Whole. Shark teeth in the backs of their head. Necks that stretch around an entire island, bloodthirsty. Hungry for babies and pregnant women. Monsters.

My three-year-old likes to hunt for monsters in our closet. We use the light of my cell phone. A blue glow in the dark. We whisper to each other – did you hear that?

Did I hear what?

The silence of my dreams is severed by her screaming nightmares. And I am a mewling mess turned monster huddled in the corner wide-eyed, wild haired, unable to touch, unable to care, unable to bear the exhaustion, anxiety clawing away at my chest. Am I even

human? Post-partum – easier to diagnose after the fact. Two years later those memories haunt me. When I became the bump in the night. When I realized I needed to protect her. From me.

Did you hear that?

Nerik gave birth to something resembling the eggs of a sea turtle and Flora gave birth to something like intestines.

In our legends lives a monster. Woman demons, unhinged jaws. Swallowing their own babies. Driven mad. Turned flesh rotten. Blood through their eyes their teeth their nose.

Were the women who gave birth to nightmares considered monsters? Were they driven mad by these unholy things that came from their bodies? Were they sick with the feeling of horror that perhaps there was something

wrong. With them.

My three-year-old sleeps next to me. I have lost my fangs and ugly dreams. I watch her chest inhale. Exhale. Know that she is real, she is mine. I try to write forgiveness and healing into our story. Into myself.

In legends lives a woman. Turned monster from loneliness. Turned monster from agony and suns exploding in her chest. She gives birth to a child that is not so much a child but too much a jellyfish. The child is struggling for breath. Struggling in pain. She wants to bring the child peace. Bring her home. Her first home. Inside her body.
It is an embrace. It is only. An embrace. She kneels next to the body.

And inhales.

NOTE
1. Glenn Alcalay, 'The Sociocultural Impact of Nuclear Weapons Tests in the Marshall Islands', (unpublished field report: 1981), pp. 1-2.

'Give birth to nightmares': The Marshallese Nuclear Legacy and Women's Health in Kathy Jetñil-Kijiner's 'Monster'

MICHELLE KEOWN

On 1 March 1954, the world's first nuclear disaster began to unfold when the United States detonated the fifteen megaton BRAVO bomb – which was to be the largest and 'dirtiest' bomb in its Cold War arsenal – in Bikini Atoll in the Marshall Islands. Using new thermonuclear technology (which generates more explosive power than atomic bombs by fusing rather than splitting atoms), BRAVO was almost a thousand times more powerful than the atomic bombs dropped on Hiroshima and Nagasaki in 1945. It vaporized three islands on Bikini Atoll, left a mile-wide crater through the reef, and spread radioactive fallout across an area of 50,000 square miles. This article explores the legacy of BRAVO and other US nuclear tests in the Marshall Islands, beginning with a discussion of its effects on the health of Marshall Islanders (who have suffered a wide range of illnesses across generations as a result of irradiation of their bodies and environments), and then analysing representations of the nuclear legacy in the work of Marshallese poet, Kathy Jetñil-Kijiner, and artists, Munro Te Whata and Solomon Enos, with whom I collaborated in producing graphic adaptations of Jetñil-Kijiner's antinuclear poems 'History Project' and 'Monster'.

At the time of the BRAVO test, the Marshall Islands, along with other Micronesian territories seized from Japan by the US during the Second World War, were part of a UN-mandated US 'Strategic Trust Territory', a unique designation that allowed the US to use the Marshall Islands as a site for multiple Cold War nuclear tests in its race for global military dominance. Between 1946 and 1958, sixty-seven atmospheric and underwater nuclear tests were carried out within the northern atolls of Bikini and Enewetak, with devastating consequences for Marshallese peoples and their natural environment. By the time of the BRAVO detonation, the people of Bikini and Enewetak had already been relocated to other islands further south – on the understanding that their exile would be temporary – but the bomb spread radioactive fallout across inhabited atolls located downwind and east of Bikini (primarily Rongelap, Ailinginae, and Utirik atolls). The US claimed that the wind unexpectedly changed direction immediately prior to the test, resulting in unintended exposure of the islanders. However, scholarly analysis of a range of Atomic Energy Commission (AEC) documentation declassified in the 1990s revealed that military staff had at least six hours' notice that the wind was blowing towards inhabited atolls, but chose to detonate the bomb without evacuating the islanders, even though relocations had taken place for previous, smaller nuclear tests.[1] This AEC documentation was released only because an international investigation into the effects of radiation on human beings resulted in the US being compelled to share information about its testing programme with the Marshallese government.

The nuclear fallout, which was mixed with pulverized coral, resembled snowflakes falling from the sky, and local children played in it and tasted it, not realizing that it was deadly 'poison', as the radioactive particles came to be known afterwards. The people of Rongelap, Ailinginae, and Rongerik were not evacuated until several days after their exposure, and by the time they were taken south to Kwajalein atoll (the site of a US naval station, and subsequently a ballistic missile testing range that operates to this day), they were suffering various symptoms of acute radiation poisoning, including vomiting, skin lesions, and hair loss. Nuclear survivors, such as Darlene Keju-Johnson and Lijon Eknilang, who later became international advocates for Marshallese nuclear justice, have reported a range of longer-term health problems affecting not just those islanders exposed to fallout, but also subsequent generations. From the 1960s right through to the present day, many islanders have developed thyroid tumours, blood and metabolic disorders, cataracts, cancers and leukaemia, with women experiencing widespread reproductive health problems including multiple miscarriages and stillbirths, as well as birth defects in surviving children. Many women have reported giving birth to what have been termed 'jellyfish' or 'jelly' babies: small beings without bones, heads or limbs, and with transparent skin that reveals the organs underneath. Such babies typically live only for a few hours before they stop breathing. Other women have reported giving birth to organisms resembling bunches of grapes, while others have observed serious disabilities in surviving children, including musculoskeletal degeneration and lowered immunity to diseases.[2]

Many Marshall Islanders believe that they were deliberately exposed to fallout so that US scientists could study the effects of radiation on the human body. Analysis of the declassified documents released in the 1990s (which were made available online during the Clinton administration) supports this argument. This scholarly work (by anthropologists and physicians such as Holly Barker, Barbara Rose Johnston, Seiji Yamada and Matthew Akiyama) is of great importance given that much of the declassified material was subsequently removed from the internet during the George W. Bush administration.[3] The documentation reveals that shortly after the BRAVO test the people of Rongelap, Ailinginae, and Utirik were enrolled (under the guise of humanitarian aid) as human subjects in project 4.1, a US scientific study of the effects of beta and gamma radiation on human beings.[4] When the people of Rongelap returned to their contaminated atoll in 1957 (having been told by the US that it was now safe for habitation), the project 4.1 scientists monitored the effects of the consumption of contaminated local foods on the health of the islanders, some of whom had been exposed to fallout and some of whom had not (and were therefore selected as a control group). By 1961, body burdens of the radioactive isotope cesium 137 were 300 times higher in the islanders than in the bodies of the scientific research team, and although (as the health of islanders began to deteriorate) the Rongelap people petitioned the US to evacuate them to a safer site, it was the Greenpeace flagship, *Rainbow Warrior*, that eventually transported the islanders to Mejatto, a small island located within Kwajalein atoll, in 1985.[5] Seiji Yamada and Matthew Akiyama, US-based Japanese physicians who studied the declassified documents, assert that Project 4.1 scientists exposed the people of Rongelap and Utirik to further radioactive agents – chromium-51 and tritium – without their knowledge or consent in order to further explore the effects of radioisotopes in the human body.[6] A document from a 1956 AEC meeting is particularly revealing. Merril Eisenbud, director of the AEC Health and Safety Laboratory, is recorded as saying:

> Now that Island [Utirik] ... is by far the most contaminated place in the world and it will be very interesting to go back and get good environmental data ... so as to get a measure of the human uptake when people live in a contaminated environment. Now, data of this type has never been available. While it is true that these people do not live, I would say, the way Westerners do, civilized people, it is nevertheless also true that these people are more like us than mice.[7]

This is a stark manifestation of biocolonialism – a practice that extends extractive colonialism into the realm of the human body.[8] Project 4.1 is deeply imbricated in the broader context of the colonial exploitation of the Marshall Islands by the United States since the Second World War.

The unique designation of the Trust Territory of the Pacific (comprising the Marshall Islands, the Mariana Islands, and the Caroline Islands) as a 'strategic' trust meant that its administrator was answerable to the UN Security Council, where the United States had a veto, rather than the UN General Assembly. This allowed the US to prevent visitors from other countries from travelling to the Marshall Islands on grounds of national security (a practice known as 'strategic denial'), and to restrict the travel of islanders, while it undertook its nuclear testing programme.[9] There was very little investment in the socio-economic 'development' of the islands in the decades following the war: urban areas, roads, port facilities, and other infrastructure were left to deteriorate, and by the early 1960s, the per capita income of Micronesians was only a third of what it had been under the Japanese colonial administration.[10] This created a situation of economic dependency that paved the way for the 1986 Compact of Free Association, which enabled a continuing neo-colonial relationship between the US and the Marshall Islands in spite of the islands becoming a Republic at this point, having achieved self-governing status in 1979. Further, the displacement of islanders from the irradiated northern atolls and from Kwajalein (site of a US ballistic missile testing base, as noted above) contributed to an unsustainable increase in the populations of the two main urban centres, Majuro and Ebeye. Ebeye's population of over 15,000 people is located on an island of a mere 0.14 square miles in surface area, with many of its residents displaced from various neighbouring islands in Kwajalein atoll that are now controlled by the US military. Many residents of Ebeye travel to Kwajalein daily to engage in low-paid, largely menial work for the US military and their families. They are forced to carry identification documents and to return to Ebeye each evening, and are denied access to the heavily subsidized supermarket products and high-quality healthcare enjoyed by the Americans. By contrast, healthcare in Majuro and Ebeye (not to mention the lesser populated or 'outer' islands) is severely underfunded, and islanders are heavily dependent on imported, expensive foods, resulting in high diabetes rates alongside widespread problems with other non-communicable and communicable diseases, poverty, unemployment, teenage pregnancy and substance abuse.[11]

Across the decades following the nuclear testing, Marshall Islanders have vigorously petitioned the US to decontaminate their islands and adequately compensate their communities for the major displacements and health problems they have suffered under US hegemony. Some limited compensation has been paid to members of the four atolls

(Rongelap, Utirik, Enewetak and Bikini) officially recognized by the US as having been directly affected by nuclear testing, but scientific evidence has shown that nuclear fallout spread throughout the Marshall Islands during the testing era, with a resulting detrimental impact on the health of people throughout the islands. Some resettlement of Enewetak took place after a partial cleanup by the US in the late 1970s (involving the removal of contaminated topsoil and debris), but most of the islands in the atoll are still uninhabitable, and the Bikini people exist in near-permanent exile, with their atoll estimated to remain uninhabitable for at least 24,000 years unless substantial funds for decontamination and reconstruction are secured.[12] Under the 1986 Compact of Free Association agreement, a $150 million reparations fund was established for the four 'nuclear atolls', and in 1998 the RMI (Republic of the Marshall Islands) Nuclear Claims Tribunal began investigating and awarding compensation for personal injury and property damage.[13] However, these funds have proved grossly inadequate: the Tribunal ruled that over $2 billion was owed to claimants, but was unable to pay over the vast majority of this once the reparations fund was exhausted.

The campaign for nuclear justice has continued into the twenty-first century; in 2014, for example, the Marshall Islands attempted to bring to the International Court of Justice (ICJ) legal cases against nine countries (including the US) for failing to comply with the 1968 nuclear non-proliferation treaty, but was only permitted to bring cases against three countries (India, Pakistan, and the UK), as the other six countries did not recognize the court's jurisdiction. The ICJ eventually dismissed the cases in 2016 on the grounds that there was no evidence of the Marshall Islands having a prior dispute with any of the three countries in question. In 2017, a UN Treaty on the prohibition of nuclear weapons was finally adopted by a majority of member states, but at the time of writing this article, the Treaty was still not in force and, ominously, not only had the US not ratified the Treaty, but the Marshall Islands were also absent from the list of ratifying signatories in spite of supporting the Treaty back in 2017.[14]

Kathy Jetñil-Kijiner, a Marshallese poet and eco-activist who has played a key role in the ongoing campaign for nuclear justice, has speculated that this change in policy regarding the 2017 Treaty is likely 'tied directly to our relationship to the US, and to provisions in our Compact that make it challenging for our country to confront the US on nuclear issues'.[15] As she points out, funding from the US 'constitutes a huge portion' of RMI's annual budget, and with the 1986 Compact granting Marshall Islanders the right to live and work in the US, thousands of islanders who have travelled there (many in search of better healthcare to treat illnesses resulting from the nuclear testing) are in a vulnerable position in view of Trump-era hostilities towards 'communities of color'.[16]

Jetñil-Kijiner's support of the Marshallese campaign for nuclear justice dates back at least as far as her high school education in Honolulu (where she grew up) in the early 2000s, when she chose to undertake a history project on US nuclear testing that later formed the focus of a performance poem, 'History Project', about which I have written extensively elsewhere.[17] 'History Project' is one of a number of poems by Jetñil-Kijiner that explore both the environmental and human costs of US nuclear colonialism alongside other challenges facing the Marshall Islands. These include ill-health resulting from the high reliance on imported processed foods, as well various climate change impacts affecting the low-lying Marshall Islands (which average only two metres above sea level), such as increasingly extreme weather, rising sea levels, and coral bleaching.[18]

A particularly striking feature of Jetñil-Kijiner's antinuclear poetry is her exploration of the radically detrimental impact of radiation exposure on Marshallese women's health. In 'History Project', Jetñil-Kijiner juxtaposes official US records of the nuclear testing with the testimonies of irradiated Marshallese women who have given birth to 'jelly babies' and suffered multiple miscarriages, which they were too ashamed to reveal to their husbands – partly because within Marshallese culture, as Rongelapese nuclear activist, Lijon Eknilang, has pointed out, reproductive problems are widely believed to result from women being unfaithful to their husbands.[19] Jetñil-Kijiner acknowledges this poignant nexus between nuclear violence and gender politics explicitly, switching into italics while maintaining her first-person perspective in order to embody and honour the voices of her female compatriots: '*I thought it was my fault / I thought / there must be something / wrong / inside me*'.[20]

Jetñil-Kijiner offers an even more personal exploration of the impact of nuclear colonialism on Marshallese women's health in her 2017 poem, 'Monster', published in this issue of *Moving Worlds* and initially posted on her blog in January 2018.[21] She undertook extensive research before writing the poem, consulting the work of anthropologists and historians; the testimonies of Eknilang and other Marshallese women affected by reproductive health problems; and Marshallese traditional stories focused on the figure of the mejenkwaad, a female demon that features prominently in the poem. The mejenkwaad, as Jetñil-Kijiner observes, is one of the most 'ominous' figures in the Marshallese oral tradition, with a propensity for devouring pregnant women, babies, and even whole islands.[22] A traditional story from Enewetak printed in Jack A. Tobin's *Stories from the Marshall Islands* – one of Jetñil-Kijiner's main sources, comprising narratives recounted to Tobin by Marshallese elders between 1950 and 1975 – outlines many of the key characteristics of the mejenkwaad. Notably, pregnant women, those who die in childbirth, or women whose babies have not yet reached their first birthday, are customarily considered to be vulnerable to being possessed by (or transformed into) mejenkwaad, particularly if they spend time alone.[23] Such women, the Enewetak narrative reveals, can become physically terrifying:

> A mouth can open up at the base of the affected person's neck. ...The neck can expand and stretch out to another island. ... Blood flows from between the teeth of the affected person. The eyes are wild and insane looking. The place at the back of the neck moves as if it is breathing.[24]

Jetñil-Kijiner references these horrifying attributes in her poem but, intriguingly, she also develops an extended conceit based on conversations she has had with family members who

> theorized that the mejenkwaad legend might have been created to discuss postpartum depression – that it was a way in which our ancestors tried to understand the deep sadness that can translate into a sort of madness after the initial trauma or birth.[25]

As she observes, Tobin makes a related point in a note accompanying a mejenkwaad story from Kwajalein: he argues that the '*mejenkwaad* concept may be based upon anxieties of women (and their relatives) during pregnancy. The mortality rate of both mothers and babies may have been quite high'.[26]

Jetñil-Kijiner weaves these theories into an intensely poignant personal testimony in her poem, which explores her own experience of post-natal depression following the birth of her first child, a daughter. She recalls experiencing feelings of anger, helplessness, and panic throughout the first two years of her child's life (particularly at night when her daughter 'wouldn't stop crying' and experienced 'screaming nightmares'). These experiences, she argues, transformed her into a 'mewling mess turned monster huddled in the corner', and made her feel like she had become a danger to her own child, like the mejenkwaad who had a reputation for devouring her own progeny.[27]

However, Jetñil-Kijiner extends this personal trauma into the broader context of the spectrum of reproductive health problems suffered by

Marshallese women in the wake of nuclear testing, alternating in the early lines of the poem between a more clinical enumeration of statistics ('574 – the number of stillbirths and miscarriages after the bombs of 1951. Before the bombs? 52'), and on the other hand, an empathetic engagement with the effects of these reproductive problems on women's mental health: 'Were the women who gave birth to nightmares considered monsters? Were they driven mad by these unholy things that came from their bodies?'[28] Significantly, she draws on the testimonies of Eknilang and others who compared their deformed offspring to phenomena from their familiar natural environment, such as octopuses, turtles, jellyfish, and the eggs and viscera of animals.[29] Jetñil-Kijiner references these testimonies in an italicized sentence that appears three times in the poem: *'Nerik gave birth to something resembling the eggs of a sea turtle and Flora gave birth to something like intestines.'*[30] The repeating refrain conveys both the horror and the pathos of the experiences of these women, referenced as a form of intergenerational trauma that repeats itself within each new generation, with cell damage to the original radiation exposure victims resulting in genetic aberrations passed from grandparent to parent to child.[31]

In a radical rhetorical move, Jetñil-Kijiner relates the grief experienced by these women to the mejenkwaad's impulse to devour her own children, speculating in her notes accompanying the poem that she was experimenting with a hypothetical question: 'what if the mejenkwaad was not eating her child as a brutal act – but was instead attempting to return her child to her body ... to her first home?'[32] In developing this theory, the poem ends with a moving humanization of the mejenkwaad, figured now as a woman 'turned monster from loneliness' and 'agony', having just given birth to a 'jellyfish' baby. The mejenkwaad observes that the child is in 'pain' and 'struggling for breath', and decides to bring her 'peace' by bringing her back to her 'first home. Inside her body'. The act of swallowing the child's body is represented not as a monstrous one but rather as an 'embrace', a neo-Kristevan act that returns the suffering child to the chora/womb.[33]

Significantly, twice in the poem Jetñil-Kijiner uses heliotropes, making reference to the 'sun exploding' inside the bodies of Marshall Islanders. These heliotropes encapsulate both the violence of the nuclear detonation and the fear and grief experienced by those exposed to radiation. These heliotropes are laden with symbolic weight, indexing the widespread practice within US atomic discourse of comparing the power released by the nuclear bomb to the radiation emitted by the sun, but also the experiences of terrified Rongelapese who witnessed the BRAVO explosion and mistook it for a second sunrise inexplicably manifesting on the western horizon.[34] As Elizabeth DeLoughrey notes, in the early years of the US nuclear programme, American politicians, journalists, and other commentators invoked tropes of 'a new dawn, a rising sun, and the birth of a new world', positing the bomb as the 'product of a new kind of divinity' achieved through technological innovation.[35] This spurious naturalization of technological violence contrasts radically with the recognition by the Rongelap people that the BRAVO detonation was a profoundly *un*natural event, thereafter known as the 'day of two suns'.[36] In Jetñil-Kijiner's poem, the heliotrope also signifies the corporeal damage and ensuing physical and mental illnesses experienced by islanders exposed to fallout (as well as their descendants), and at the end of the poem, the mejenkwaad's intense grief, experienced on behalf of all Marshallese women bearing the weight of the nuclear legacy, is encapsulated in the image of the sun 'exploding in her chest'.[37]

In various funded projects, I have collaborated with Kathy and two indigenous Pacific artists in making what Rob Nixon terms the 'slow violence' of nuclear imperialism 'visible' by transforming some of her antinuclear poetry into graphic adaptations.[38] In 2016, with Kathy's permission and University of Edinburgh funding, I undertook the textual adaptation and storyboarding of 'History Project', which Maori-Niuean artist, Munro Te Whata, then transformed into a comic.[39] Because neither I nor Munro are Marshallese, we avoided explicit representations of the 'jelly babies' and other reproductive health problems described in the poem, opting instead for a silhouetted (and therefore anonymized) image of a pregnant woman against a white backdrop suggestive of the sudden flash of a nuclear explosion (see figure 1).[40] This image prefigures the heliotropic references in 'Monster', which was incorporated into a second graphic adaptation in 2017, when I worked in partnership with Kathy, indigenous Hawaiian artist, Solomon Enos, and a team of Marshallese elders and oral historians in producing a four-part graphic novel entitled *Jerakiaarlap: A Marshallese Epic*.[41]

Jerakiaarlap opens with graphic adaptations of two traditional stories focused on the seafaring heritage of the Marshall Islands, before moving on to an adaptation of 'Monster', and ending with a futuristic 'cli-fi' narrative depicting exiled Marshall Islanders returning to a rejuvenated homeland raised well above sea level through biotechnology. The 'Monster' section is the emotional core of the text, acknowledging the massive rupture in Marshallese history and culture caused by the nuclear testing, but the graphic novel situates this violent trauma within a longer *durée* that records the mobility, resilience, and adaptability of Marshall Islanders across centuries of oceanic history. The final section of the novel, a narrative of Enos's own original composition, was conceived as a 'balm of hope', depicting a future in which the wounds of nuclear testing (which has left such poisonous legacies both for the Marshallese environment and for the people of these islands and atolls) have been healed, and a return to a revitalized Majuro has become possible for those thousands of Marshall Islanders exiled through nuclear displacement and climate change.[42] Here, the balance between humans and their environment witnessed in the first two sections of the graphic novel is restored.

Contrastingly, the 'Monster' section of the graphic novel is anthropocentric, focused on the hubris of the US nuclear project and its devastating effects on the bodies of Marshall Islanders. Kathy gave us permission to reproduce her poem in full in this section of the text, and therefore Enos's adaptation is wordless (unlike in other parts of the graphic novel where images are accompanied by captions), finding visual equivalents for the rich imagery evident in the original poem. Enos's colour palette in the 'Monster' section is visceral, with dominant fleshy and magenta shades that contrast with the oceanic blue and green tones used elsewhere in the text. Furthermore a visual reference to the 'day of two suns' is included in the opening panel, which features an isolated figure standing on a beach, witnessing a sunrise in the east and a nuclear

Figure 1 below: *from* History Project: A Marshall Islands Nuclear Story
Image by Munro Te Whata with kind permission

explosion in the west, against a backdrop of sickly yellow sky (see figure 2). The adaptation also carries repeating images of a dead turtle with exposed intestines, obliquely referencing birth defects through visual equivalents of the metaphors used in the poem, but there are also more explicit visual references to the 'monster babies' described by Eknilang and others.

On the final page of the adaptation, Enos includes arresting images of white men, suggestive of the Project 4.1 scientists, with lamprey-like mouths opening at the backs of their heads; this visual allusion resonates with Marshallese descriptions of the mejenkwaad and thereby implies that the scientists too are 'monsters' directly implicated in the horrific consequences of nuclear imperialism (see figure 3).[43] This panel echoes one that appears earlier in the adaptation, where the same scientists, this time without monstrous features, are walking away from a soap dispenser emblazoned with the US flag but overlaid with rivulets of blood. Here Enos echoes the biblical imagery Jetñil-Kijiner uses in the poem, where she describes testimonies given by Marshallese women at the UN as being addressed to 'a committee of men' who, Pilate-like, 'washed their hands of this sin'. It is worth noting at this point that Marshall Islanders are among the most Christianized peoples in the world,[44] and Jetñil-Kijiner also uses biblical imagery throughout 'History Project' to reflect upon the irony of the fact that the US appealed to the Bikini Islanders' sense of Christian duty in persuading them to leave their homeland, arguing that the US nuclear testing was being performed 'for the good of mankind and to end all world wars'.[45]

The final panel of Enos's graphic adaptation offers perhaps the most arresting visual equivalent of the verbal imagery Jetñil-Kijiner draws from the testimonies of Marshallese women who witnessed severe birth defects in their babies (see figure 4). Here, the mejenkwaad is depicting seated upon ovoid coral heads, giving birth to jellyfish and poised to eat them as they emerge. Some of the jellyfish, however, are floating up past her towards the surface of the ocean, their shapes suggestive of the mushroom clouds produced by the US nuclear detonations. The spherical shapes that abound in this panel are richly suggestive of pregnancy and conception (with the jellyfish babies resembling eggs released from ovaries), but also resonate with images earlier in Enos's adaptation, where the mejenkwaad's mouth closes on human prey and then resolves into a grey semicircle that resembles the Runit Dome – a bomb crater in Enewetak atoll that was filled with nuclear waste and topped with concrete by the US navy during the partial 'cleanup' in the 1970s. The Dome is now cracked and leaking

Figure 2 top: *from Jerakiaarlap p. 60 – the yellow sky with sunrise and nuclear explosion.*

Figure 3 left: *from Jerakiaarlap p. 70 – the back of men's heads with the weird-looking mouths in their heads.*

Figure 4 bottom: *from Jerakiaarlap p. 70 – the demon-woman figure giving birth to, and eating her eggs.*

All images by Solomon Enos with kind permission

radioactive waste into Enewetak lagoon, where it drifts downwind to inhabited areas and is damaging the health of residents. Jetñil-Kijiner's poem 'Anointed', written shortly after 'Monster', again uses reproductive imagery, in this case to evoke the vitality of Runit Island prior to the nuclear testing era. As I have noted elsewhere, the Dome is represented both as a 'tomb' representing the nuclear 'death' of the island, and as an 'empty belly' that is contrasted with the rounded abdomens of 'women who could swim pregnant for miles beneath a full moon'.[46]

To conclude: as I have demonstrated, the poetry of Kathy Jetñil-Kijiner, and the graphic adaptations of her work produced by fellow indigenous Pacific artists, offer compelling creative explorations of what Clare Barker describes (in the Editorial to this issue) as 'the entanglement of medicine with the processes and infrastructure of globalization; and the connections between environment, ecology, and health in a climate changing world'. US military imperialism has imbricated Marshall Islanders in two interrelated processes of globalization, enfolding Micronesians in the US quest for world military dominance, but also, through nuclear displacement and the 1986 Compact agreement, precipitating Marshall Islanders into the large-scale international migrant flows of the late twentieth century.[47] Many of these migrants have travelled to Hawai'i and the continental US in search of adequate medical treatment for the intergenerational health problems resulting from US nuclear imperialism, and Jetñil-Kijiner's poetry offers an intense and moving exploration of the emotional as well as physical burdens carried by the Marshallese people as a result of this experience. She has lost several of her own close family members to radiogenic illnesses, and in her 2017 poetry collection, she incorporates a poignant series of poems reflecting upon the death of her niece as a result of leukaemia, and her grandmother through cancer. She argues that poetry 'brings humanity', 'touches people', and conveys 'stories we remember' in a way that bald facts and statistics cannot, and reveals that she deliberately chose performance poetry and videopoems (widely available on the internet) as a means by which to raise international awareness about the history and legacy of nuclear testing in the Marshall Islands, and the ongoing campaign for nuclear justice.[48] The graphic adaptations of Jetñil-Kijiner's poetry I have discussed in this article have been produced in support of that agenda, making the 'slow violence' of nuclear imperialism visible to a global audience in a new creative nexus between poetry, art, politics and praxis.

NOTES

1. Holly Barker, *Bravo for the Marshallese: Regaining Control in a Post-nuclear, Post-colonial World* (Belmont, CA: Thomson Wadsworth, 2004); Barbara Rose Johnston, 'Nuclear Disaster: The Marshall Islands Experience and Lessons for a Post-Fukushima World', in *Global Ecologies and the Environmental Humanities: A Postcolonial Approach*, eds, Elizabeth DeLoughrey, Jill Didur and Anthony Carrigan (London and New York: Routledge, 2015), pp. 140-61.

2. Lijon Eknilang, 'Learning from Rongelap's Pain', in *Pacific Women Speak Out for Independence and Denuclearisation*, ed., Zohl de Ishtar (Annandale: Women's International League for Peace and Freedom, 1998), pp. 21-6; Darlene Keju-Johnson, 'Ebeye, Marshall Islands', in *Pacific Women Speak*, eds, Women Working for a Nuclear-free and Independent Pacific (Oxford: Green Line, 1987), pp. 6-10; Johnston, 'Nuclear Disaster'.

3. Barker, *Bravo for the Marshallese*; Johnston, 'Nuclear Disaster'; Seiji Yamada and Matthew Akiyama, '"For the good of mankind": The Legacy of Nuclear Testing in Micronesia', *Social Medicine*, 8:2 (2014) 83-92.

4. Johnston, 'Nuclear Disaster'.

5. Keju-Johnson, 'Ebeye, Marshall Islands', p. 10.

6. Yamada and Akiyama, '"For the good of mankind"', p. 86.

7. Atomic Energy Commission, *Minutes of the Advisory Committee on Biology and Medicine, January 13-14* (New York: AEC, 1956), cited in Yamada and Akiyama, '"For the good of mankind"', p. 85; and Johnston, 'Nuclear Disaster', p. 146.

8. See Clare Barker, '"The Ancestors Within": Genetics, Biocolonialism, and Medical Ethics in Patricia Grace's *Baby No-Eyes*', *Journal of Literary and Cultural Disability Studies*, 7:2 (2013) 141-58; and Laurelyn Whitt, *Science, Colonialism, and Indigenous Peoples: The Cultural Politics of Law and Knowledge* (Cambridge: Cambridge UP, 2009).

9. John C. Dorrance, *The United States and the Pacific Islands* (Westport, CT: Praeger, 1992), p. 75.

10. Dorrance, *The United States and the Pacific Islands*, p. 75.

11. Sasha Davis, *Empire's Edge: Militarization, Resistance, and Transcending Hegemony in the Pacific* (Athens, GA: U of Georgia P, 2015), p. 40.

12. Johnston, 'Nuclear Disaster', p. 148.

13. Johnston, 'Nuclear Disaster', p. 148.

14. See 'Treaties', *United Nations Office for Disarmament Affairs (UNODA)*, <http://disarmament.un.org/treaties/t/tpnw>.

15. Kathy Jetñil-Kijiner, 'New Year, New Monsters, New Poems' blogpost, *Kathy Jetñil-Kijiner*, 25 January 2018, <http://edin.ac/2MOGu5S>.

16. Jetñil-Kijiner, 'New Year, New Monsters, New Poems'.

17. Michelle Keown, 'Children of Israel: US Military Imperialism and Marshallese Migration in the Poetry of Kathy Jetnil-Kijiner', *Interventions*, 19:7 (2017) 930-47; Michelle Keown, 'War and Redemption: Militarism, Religion and Anti-Colonialism in Pacific Literature', in *Anglo-American Imperialism and the Pacific*, eds, Michelle Keown, Andrew Taylor and Mandy Treagus (London and New York: Routledge, 2018), pp. 25-48.

18. See Kathy Jetñil-Kijiner, *Iep Jaltok: Poems from a Marshallese Daughter* (Tucson: U of Arizona P, 2017).

19. International Court of Justice, 'Testimony of Lijon Eknilang to the International Court of Justice', Hague, 14 November 1995, <https://edin.ac/36uol8I>, pp. 24-28, p. 27.

20. Jetñil-Kijiner, 'History Project', *Iep Jaltok*, p. 21.

21. See Jetñil-Kijiner, 'New Year, New Monsters, New Poems'.

22. Jetñil-Kijiner, 'New Year, New Monsters, New Poems'.
23. Jack A. Tobin, *Stories from the Marshall Islands* (Honolulu: U of Hawai'i P, 2002), p. 192.
24. Tobin, *Stories from the Marshall Islands*, p. 192.
25. Jetñil-Kijiner, 'New Year, New Monsters, New Poems'.
26. Tobin, *Stories from the Marshall Islands*, p. 188.
27. Jetñil-Kijiner, 'Monster', *Moving Worlds: A Journal of Transcultural Writings*, 19:2 (2019), pp. 139-140.
28. Jetñil-Kijiner, 'Monster', p. 140.
29. ICJ, 'Testimony of Lijon Eknilang', p. 27; Jane Dibblin, *Day of Two Suns: Nuclear Testing and the Pacific Islanders* ([1988]; New York: New Amsterdam Books, 1990), p. 36.
30. Jetñil-Kijiner, 'Monster', p. 140.
31. See Dibblin, *Day of Two Suns*, p. 38.
32. Jetñil-Kijiner, 'New Year, New Monsters, New Poems'.
33. Jetñil-Kijiner, 'Monster', p. 140. See also Michelle Keown, 'Waves of Destruction: Nuclear Imperialism and Anti-nuclear Protest in the Indigenous Literatures of the Pacific', *Journal of Postcolonial Writing*, 54:5 (2018), 585-600, p. 595.
34. Elizabeth DeLoughrey, 'Heliotropes: Solar Ecologies and Pacific Radiations', in *Postcolonial Ecologies: Literatures of the Environment*, eds, Elizabeth DeLoughrey and George B. Handley (Oxford: Oxford UP, 2011), pp. 235-53, p. 246; Dibblin, *Day of Two Suns*; Keown, 'War and Redemption'.
35. DeLoughrey, 'Heliotropes', p. 246.
36. Barker, *Bravo for the Marshallese*, p. 90; Dibblin, *Day of Two Suns*, p. 25; Keown, 'War and Redemption', pp. 38-9.
37. Jetñil-Kijiner, 'Monster', p. 140.
38. See Rob Nixon, *Slow Violence and the Environmentalism of the Poor* (Cambridge, MA: Harvard UP, 2011).
39. Kathy Jetñil-Kijiner, Michelle Keown, and Munro Te Whata, *History Project: A Marshall Islands Nuclear Story* (Pohnpei: Island Research and Education Initiative, 2018).
40. This image is also discussed in Keown, 'Waves of Destruction'.
41. Solomon Enos, Kathy Jetñil-Kijiner, Alson Kelen, Michelle Keown, and Rain Senight, *Jerakiaarlap: A Marshall Islands Epic* (Pohnpei: Island Research and Education Initiative, 2019). *Jerakiaarlap* was produced with funding from the Economic and Social Research Council (ESRC) and the Arts and Humanities Research Council (AHRC) under the Global Challenges Research Fund (GCRF).
42. Michelle Keown and Shari Sabeti, unpublished interview with Solomon Enos, Honolulu, 25 April 2019.
43. See also Keown and Sabeti, unpublished interview.
44. Francis X. Hezel, *Strangers in Their Own Land: A Century of Colonial Rule in the Caroline and Marshall Islands* (Honolulu: U of Hawai'i P, 1995).
45. Jetñil-Kijiner, 'History Project'. See also Jack Niedenthal, *For the Good of Mankind: A History of the People of Bikini and their Islands* (Majuro: Bravo, 2001); and Keown, 'War and Redemption'.
46. Keown, 'Waves of Destruction', pp. 595-6.
47. Keown, 'Children of Israel', p. 931.
48. Kathy Jetñil-Kijiner, interview with Fourth Branch, <www.youtube.com/watch?v=pjGrSu22v58>; 'Fighting Climate Change with Poems: Kathy Jetnil-Kijiner', <www.youtube.com/watch?v=65nhhzhZ_x8>. Many of Jetñil-Kijiner's videopoems are accessible on her blog site at <http://edin.ac/2MOGu5S>.

Notes on Contributors

A recipient of many prizes and awards, **Simon Armitage** has published twelve collections of poems, including *The Unaccompanied* (2017) and *Sandettie Light Vessel Automatic* (2019); two novels; translations of medieval literature such as the highly acclaimed *Sir Gawain and the Green Knight* (2007); and non-fiction works, among them *Walking Home* (2012) and *Walking Away* (2015). His other works include TV films, radio docu-drama, and theatre plays. He is Professor of Poetry at Leeds University; was Professor of Poetry at Oxford University in 2015-2019; and is the current national Poet Laureate.

Clare Barker is Associate Professor in English Literature at Leeds University. She is the author of *Postcolonial Fiction and Disability: Exceptional Children, Metaphor and Materiality* (2011); and co-editor of *The Cambridge Companion to Literature and Disability* (2017), and two special issues of the *Journal of Literary and Cultural Disability Studies*, 'Disabling Postcolonialism' (2010) and 'Disability and Indigeneity' (2013). Her current research project – Genetics and Biocolonialism in Contemporary Literature and Film – was funded by a Wellcome Trust Seed Award.

Veronica Barnsley is Lecturer in Contemporary Literature at the University of Sheffield. Her research focuses on global childhoods at the intersection of postcolonial studies, childhood studies, and international development. She also has interests in medical humanities and is currently part of an interdisciplinary project on mental health interventions in Uganda.

Michelle Chiang is Assistant Professor in English at Nanyang Technological University, Singapore. Her published research focuses on the intersection between Literature and the Philosophy of Time. She is the author of *Beckett's Intuitive Spectator: Me to play* (Palgrave, 2018). Her current projects are: Time of the Absurd; and Death Memoirs: The Experience of Time in Stories of the Dying.

Frances Hemsley is a Teaching Associate in World Literatures at the University of Bristol. Her research focuses on African and postcolonial literary studies, and on intersections between these fields and the medical and environmental humanities.

Katherine Storm Hindley is Assistant Professor in English at Nanyang Technological University, Singapore. She holds first degrees from Oxford and a PhD from Yale. Her research interests lie at the intersection of medieval literature, manuscript studies, and the history of medicine. She is currently completing a monograph on the use of text for protection and healing in medieval England.

Michelle Keown is Professor of Pacific and Postcolonial Literature at the University of Edinburgh. She has published widely on Indigenous Pacific and Postcolonial Literature and is the author of *Postcolonial Pacific Writing* (2005) and *Pacific Islands Writing* (2007) and the co-editor of *Comparing Postcolonial Diasporas* (2010) and *Anglo-American Imperialism and the Pacific* (2018).

Kathy Jetñil-Kijiner, a Marshall Islander poet, performance artist, and educator, received international acclaim through her poetry performance at the 2014 UN Climate Summit in New York. Her collection of poetry, *Iep Jāltok: Poems from a Marshallese Daughter*, was published in 2017. Kathy co-founded the youth environmentalist non-profit Jo-Jikum, dedicated to empowering Marshallese youth to seek solutions to climate change and other environmental impacts threatening their home island.

Madeleine Lee is an investment manager who also writes poetry. She has published ten volumes of poems, the latest being *the size of azuki beans*, an English-Chinese bilingual volume. She has been writer-in-residence at Singapore Botanic Gardens and National Gallery of Singapore and is currently WIR to Nature Society/Bird Life International. Madeleine's works are also widely anthologized.

Graham Matthews is Assistant Professor in English at Nanyang Technological University, Singapore. His most recent book is *Will Self and Contemporary British Society* and his work on contemporary literature has appeared in journals and edited collections including *Modern Fiction Studies, Textual Practice, Journal of Modern Literature, Literature & Medicine, Critique*, and *The Cambridge Companion to British Postmodern Fiction.*

Avaes Mohammad is a writer working across forms. His scripts chronicle post 9/11 multicultural Britain. As a poet his influences range from the Sufi Saints of South Asia to the Dub Poets of Jamaica. His essays and opinion pieces in the national press are examples of critical thought leadership.

Amy Rushton is Lecturer at Nottingham Trent University; her research intersects with postcolonial studies, world-literature, and queer theory. Her current project explores the relationship between narratives of depression and colonialism in American and African literatures. Recent publications include essays on Afropolitan fiction and utopianism, and depression in contemporary fiction and pop music. Amy leads the World-Literature Network's Mental Health research cluster.

Emily Kate Timms is a PhD student in the School of English at the University of Leeds, UK. Her thesis examines postcolonial representations of age and ageing in Aotearoa New Zealand and Caribbean fiction and film. Her work is sponsored by the White Rose College of the Arts and Humanities. She is the editorial assistant for *Moving Worlds: A Journal of Transcultural Writings.*